Just Add Water

Making the City of Chicago

Renee Kreczmer

LAKE CLAREMONT PRESS

an imprint of Everything Goes Media

Chicago ■ Milwaukee

Just Add Water: Making the City of Chicago
Renee Kreczmer

Published June 2012 by:

LAKE CLAREMONT PRESS

an imprint of Everything Goes Media, LLC
lcp@lakeclaremont.com
www.lakeclaremont.com

Publisher's Cataloging-In-Publication Data
(Prepared by The Donohue Group, Inc.)

Kreczmer, Renee.
    Just add water : making the city of Chicago / Renee Kreczmer.

        p. : ill. (some col.), maps, charts, facsims. ; cm.

    Summary: Chicago history for kids taking an investigative approach, mostly for classroom/library use.
    Interest age group: 007-010.
    Includes bibliographical references and index.
    ISBN: 978-1-893121-64-5

    1. Chicago (Ill.)--History--Problems, exercises, etc.--Juvenile literature. 2. Chicago (Ill.)--Description and travel--Problems, exercises, etc.--Juvenile literature. 3. Chicago (Ill.)--History--Problems, exercises, etc. 4. Chicago (Ill.)--Description and travel--Problems, exercises, etc. I. Title.

F548.33 .K74 2012
917.731/1

18 17 16 15 14 13 12   11 10 9 8 7 6 5 4 3 2 1
Printed in the United States of America by Versa Press, Inc. of East Peoria, Illinois.

Table of Contents

Foreword

Have you ever loved learning about something? We have! Third grade Social Studies. Chicago history to be exact. A good teacher can make all the difference. Ms Kreczmer is our *good teacher.* She made it fun to learn about Chicago history. We didn't just read about Chicago history, she made us think about Chicago history. Simply providing us with the answers was not enough; instead, giving us the tools, guidance, and encouragement to research the answers together is Ms. Kreczmer's way. Social Studies time went quickly in her classroom. We looked forward to Social Studies and hoped she could cram in a few extra minutes each day to share a new picture, book, or artifact.

When Ms. Kreczmer sees us in the hall, she'll tell us about her weekend adventures and the new Chicago facts she has learned. From the Chicago History Museum in Chicago to the Illinois Waterway Visitors Center in Lockport, Ms. Kreczmer is always learning and discovering something new to share with her class and former students. Ms. Kreczmer always said "field trips made the learning come to life"; seeing and touching history made it real for us. We know that Ms. Kreczmer spends many weekends on her own field trips with her parents and dog, Pixie.

Our favorite investigations include #8, *Missing: Chicago's Downtown. Where did it go?*, and #5, *What happened here?* The pictures of things that were burned or saved from the Great Chicago Fire made a big impression on us. Ms. Kreczmer not only told us stories about families being separated and reunited, but also helped us discover how Chicago became even more prosperous after the fire occurred. When we learned the history of Fort Dearborn, Ms. Kreczmer made us feel like we knew the people involved, and we cared what happened to them. Today when we are downtown and see the street names, they remind us of the people of Fort Dearborn we learned about. By giving clues and pointing students of all ages in the right direction, Ms. Kreczmer has carefully planned investigations that can help anybody become a Chicago star. Her investigations are not confined to the classroom and encourage families and individuals to be open to learning the history of Chicago out in the world. We know you will enjoy investigating Chicago as much as we did.

—Rachael and Thomas Shaw

Preface

It has been my goal to find a way to get kids as excited about social studies as they are about science. I thought about hands-on experimenting, but that didn't lend itself to the curriculum. My teaching method that you'll encounter in this book began when I used photographs with discussion for students who didn't read well. From there, the idea of small groups making predictions during these photo presentations occurred to me. Then, the idea of analyzing cartoons, artifacts, photographs, data, and works of art surfaced and developed. Finally, it was a new science series at our school—comprised of *investigations*—that sparked the idea for the format I now use to teach local history.

A series of investigations will guide you through the fascinating history that formed the mighty city of Chicago. Each investigation opens with a question. An artifact or photograph with analysis questions will help lead you to a conclusion. You'll read the information to check your conclusion and collect stars for every correct answer. At the end of the book, you will count your stars and be judged!

Research for this book began 17 years ago, when I taught my first group of third grade students the exciting history of Chicago. I didn't know much at first, but the more I learned, the more I wanted to learn. Stored in my memory banks is information from countless tours of historic city sites and museums; books; articles; dusty old volumes at the Historical Society Research Center; classes; videos; movies; exploration trips with friends and students; emails to historians; and many, many hours surfing the web.

Writing a book was an experience I never imagined I would have, but I'm so glad to have had the opportunity! Thank you, Rachael and Thomas, for being so excited about Chicago history that my name made it to Lake Claremont Press.

I dedicate this to my past, present, and future students of Chicago history, especially Matt, Katie, Marisa, and Keira. This project was only conceived in my quest to make history more interesting for you.
And to Pixie, who has been patiently waiting for a walk for the past six months!

"I am a traveler of both time and space, to be where I have been.

To sit with elders of the gentle race, This world has seldom seen.

They talk of days for which they sit and wait, All will be revealed."

—Led Zeppelin, *Kashmir*

Introduction

Welcome, kids, to a series of adventures exploring Chicago's exciting history. Investigate the *ingredients* that went into making the city of Chicago and collect stars for your discoveries along the way.

On April 4, 1917, the Chicago City Council and Mayor William Hale Thompson approved the municipal flag of Chicago. It was designed by poet and lecturer Wallace Rice, who spent six weeks designing 300 flags before his winning design was chosen by a flag committee. The original flag had two red stars.

The flag's stars and stripes symbolize important elements in the building of Chicago. Complete the investigations in this book to unlock their secret code!

Investigation 1:

Is this a good location to build a commmunity?

The photograph shows a **prairie**[1] with a large swampy area. A swamp is a wetland area that is sometimes covered with water, and sometimes dry. Find clues in the photograph to help you answer the questions:

- What **natural resources**[2] are available?
- How could the natural resources be helpful for people?

---

[1] prairie = a large area of flat land with fertile soil and tall grasses
[2] natural resources = materials from nature that are useful to people

■ Are there any materials for building a **shelter?**[3] What are they?

■ Would it be easy or difficult to build on this land? Why? Why not?

■ Can people get food and water? How?

■ What types of animals might live here?

■ Is this good land for farming? How can you tell?

■ What types of **transportation**[4] might people use?

■ How is transportation important to a community?

The arrow on the map points out the same location shown in the photograph. Look at the map to find more clues about whether this is a good location to build a community. Before railroads and automobiles, transportation by water was the quickest way to **ship**[5] **goods**[6] and transport people from one place to another.

■ Why is it important for a community to transport people and goods?

■ Does this location have any **waterways**[7] that could be used for transportation?

---

[3] shelter = something that covers or gives protection
[4] transportation = a way of moving people or goods
[5] ship = to move goods by boat
[6] goods = natural or manufactured products like grain, fur, electronics
[7] waterway = a body of water used for travel

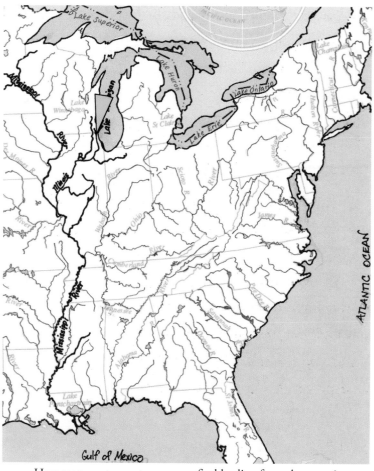

How many water routes can you find leading from the arrow?

■ By using connecting waterways, where could people go by boat?

■ Could ships reach the Gulf of Mexico? How?

■ Could ships reach the Atlantic Ocean? How?

Now make your decision!

What are the *benefits* (good things) this location has to offer? What are some of the *risks* (bad things) about the geography of this area?

Let's see. Swampland is a terrible place for building. The mud is squishy, deep, and wet for much of the year, which would make building very difficult. You wouldn't be able to dig into the mushy mud, because it would just keep filling up with water. Buildings would sink into the mud, as would you (up to your waist!) while you were trying to build. The prairie grass was

Prairie grasses at Goose Lake Prairie.

six to eight feet high all around the swamp and was difficult to cut down. The grass had very deep roots, making it also hard to dig up.

On the other hand, this location had great natural resources like good, fertile soil for growing crops. You can tell the soil is fertile, because otherwise the prairie grass and trees wouldn't have grown here. Since prairie land is flat, it is also easy to plant crops (have you seen many farms on mountains?), build homes, and raise animals. Nearby there are trees that can provide wood for building homes and fences. People also used wood to make fires for cooking and heating. The bark of trees was used for building shelters and bark canoes for traveling by water.

Animals such as buffalo, deer, wild turkeys, fish, and beavers lived in this location. These animals were hunted and used for meat, clothing, and shelter by the people of this area.

But the most important benefit of this location was the surrounding waterways. The swamp was known as Mud Lake, and when it flooded, boats could travel from Lake Michigan through the Chicago River to the Des Plaines River. Then they could travel from the Illinois River to the Mississippi River and farther without stopping. During dry times, the traveler would

The Chicago River, close to where it once fed into Lake Michigan.

only have to *portage* (carry) his boat across about one and a half miles of land to the Des Plaines River from the Chicago River—still a great shortcut!

It was for this reason—transportation—that people did decide to build a community here. Even though building on a swamp was a problem, the residents knew they would figure out a solution. Can you guess what they did? In a later investigation, you'll find out!

To the left is a photo of the community built on a swamp, located between a river and a lake. It is now known as Chicago, Illinois, but it took a lot more than a good system of waterways to make the city what it is today.

Is this a good location to build a community? Why? Why not?

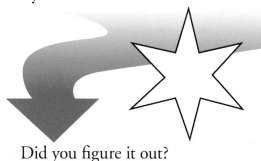

Did you figure it out?

Award yourself one star if you answered, **YES!**[8]

---

[8] If you own this book and it does not belong to a school, library, or someone else, you can color each star red that you collect for a correct answer.

This is an excellent location for a community because of the natural resources, location near waterways, and flat, fertile land for planting.

[EXPLORE THE PRAIRIE!]

Around Chicago, you can still find living prairie grasses. The largest area of surviving prairie is Goose Lake Prairie in Morris, Illinois. Explore the prairie and imagine how Chicago looked hundreds of years ago.

Goose Lake Prairie State Natural Area
5010 N. Jugtown Road
Morris, IL 60450
(815) 942-2899
www.gooselakeprairie.org

[INVESTIGATE LIMESTONE.]

Somewhat closer to Chicago is a *dolomite prairie*. Dolomite is a special kind of **limestone**[9] formed by **glaciers**[10] that melted thousands of years ago. This glacier water contained lots of calcium but very little oxygen. Limestone would become a very important natural resource in Chicago's growth. Can you predict how it was used?

Lockport Prairie Nature Preserve
Route 53 (Broadway) and Division Street,
    about 1 mile south of Route 7
Lockport, IL
(815) 727-8700
http://www.reconnectwithnature.org/preserves-trails/
    Lockport-Prairie

---

[9] limestone = a rock made of the remains of living things like coral and shells, used mainly for building
[10] glacier = a gigantic mountain of ice that moves slowly over land, carving the land as it moves

Investigation 2:

How did this little creek and this animal attract Europeans to Chicago?

Find clues in the photographs to help you answer the questions:

■ Before trains, automobiles, and airplanes, what was the fastest way to transport goods and people?

- What animals might live in this environment?
- In what ways do people use animals?
- What is this animal?
- Where does it live?
- What adaptations does the animal need to survive in its environment?
- For what purpose might people use this animal in large quantities?
- What do you notice about its coat?

Beavers needed in France! In the 1600s, the most fashionable French women draped themselves in fur. French men enjoyed wearing fancy hats made of **felted**[1] beaver **pelts.**[2] Fur from a beaver has a waterproof quality, making it excellent for outdoor wear. In France and French colonies in North America, beaver fur hats were so much in demand that the beaver was nearly **extinct**[3] in parts of Europe!

Felted beaver fur hats on display at the Isle a la Cache Museum.

Around the same time, Europeans became very interested in Asian goods like umbrellas, spices, and silk.

---

[1] felted = a process in which beaver fur was torn from the pelt and pressed flat with heat and water
[2] pelts = the skin of an animal with the fur or hair still on it
[3] extinct = describing an entire population of plants or animals that no longer exist

In France, there was a high **demand**[4] for these goods, meaning they were very valuable for sellers. Seeking a shortcut, the French government sent explorers to find a *Northwest passage* to the Pacific Ocean. If a faster route to Asia could be found, merchants who sold Asian goods in France and Canada could make a lot of money.

The French government sent explorer Louis Jolliet to find a shortcut to the *Vermilion Sea* (Pacific Ocean). Jolliet packed two canoes with supplies like gunpowder, corn, and goods for trading for his 2,500-mile, five-month-long journey. With him traveled five **voyageurs**[5] and a Jesuit priest named Father Jacques Marquette. Father Marquette had read about explorers as a boy and dreamed of one day exploring faraway lands and teaching religion to their natives.

Jolliet and Marquette met some Miami in Wisconsin who told them of a Great River (the Mississippi River). Jolliet thought it could be the shortcut to the Pacific Ocean that they were looking for, so they directed their canoes on that path. Along the way, the explorers met another tribe of natives who corrected them, letting them know that the Mississippi River led to the Gulf of Mexico and not the Pacific Ocean.

---

[4] demand = lots of people really, really wanting something badly
[5] voyageurs = men who worked for fur companies, paddled canoes, and carried 90-pound (or more) bundles of pelts and goods across portages

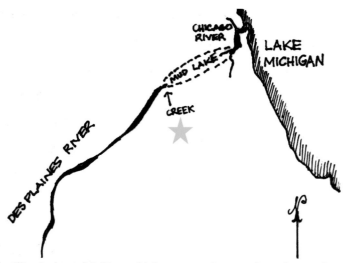

The Illinois showed Jolliet and Marquette a shortcut through a creek to get back to Canada. Before the mid-1700s, the Chicago River had no name and was referred to as a creek, stream, or ditch. The Des Plaines River was named in 1825, but before that was sometimes called the River Chekagou!

Jolliet and Marquette began their long journey home. On the way back up the Mississippi River, they met members of the Illinois tribe who guided them to a shortcut through a creek (Portage Creek). At the end of the creek was a 5.43-mile-long marsh known as Mud Lake. If the travelers were lucky, they would reach Mud Lake after a rainy period and could sail the entire length of it into a river and out into Lake Michigan. However, if it were a dry season, they couldn't do that. The men would have to **portage**[6] their birch-bark canoes across the muddy land and

---

[6] portage = to carry across land from waterway to waterway

marsh, in waist-high mud, until they reached waters high enough to paddle their canoes again.

The area, where a small "stream" led into the lake, had been named *Chicagou* by the Potawatomi living around the area. The "stream" is what we call the Chicago River, and the lake is Lake Michigan. Chicagou came from the Potawatomi word, *chi-goug*, for the wild onion that grew along the banks of the **river.**[7]

Animal pelts.

Father Marquette was happy to find what he was looking for. He returned many times to the area until he died of a type of flu (probably cholera) in 1675. Jolliet, even though he did not find a water route to

[7] Hubbard, pp. 40–41

Asia, returned to France with good news. He reported to his government that "a bark [canoe] could go from Lake Erie to the Gulf if a canal of half a **league**[8] were cut at the Chicago Portage,"[9] making trade with the natives easy. Jolliet also informed France of all the animals living in the area. A huge beaver dam divided Mud Lake into two parts. Beaver fur was the most valued fur, but other animals such as deer, fox, rabbit, and muskrat were also hunted for fur by natives.

Deerskin dresses.

---

[8] league = an old unit of measurement originally meaning how far a person or horse could walk in an hour, usually about three miles

[9] Quaife, pp. 4–5

Tricks or Treaties?

How did the United States take possession of the Chicago area?

Since the Revolutionary War in 1776, the United States government has made hundreds of treaties with different Native American nations. A treaty is a legal document, kind of like a contract. In the treaties, the native groups agreed to give up land for goods and money. After eight months of discussions, on August 3, 1795, a treaty was signed at Fort Greene Ville (Ohio) "between the United States of America, and the tribes of Indians called the Wyandots, Delawares, Shawanees, Ottawas, Chippewas, Pattawatimas, Miamis, Eel Rivers, Weas, Kickapoos, Piankeshaws, and Kaskaskias." The native groups agreed to give up the southern two-thirds of Ohio to the United States. The treaty also included "one piece of land six miles square, at the mouth of Chikago river, emptying into the southwest end of lake Michigan, where a fort formerly stood." Seven tribes including the Potawatomi were paid $1,000, and five other tribes received only $500 each, along with yearly goods from the United States. This was known as the Treaty of Greenville.

The Treaty of St. Louis on August 24, 1816, gave Ottawa, Chippewa, and Potawatomi tribes land ten miles north and ten miles south of the mouth of the Chicago River to the United States. The portage creek was included in the treaty.

The Treaty of Chicago with the Chippewa, Ottawa, and Potawatomi tribes was made on September 26, 1833. The native groups gave up five million acres in Chicago, Wisconsin, and Michigan in exchange for the same amount of land west of the Mississippi River.

What was tricky about these treaties?

Treaties were unfair to native tribes most of the time. Natives didn't understand how valuable the land was to Americans, and received much less for the land than it was worth. Sometimes chiefs would make treaty agreements with the United States to give away land that didn't belong to them. Language was a problem too. Native groups used *interpreters* (people who spoke both English and the native language) to deal with Americans. The interpreters weren't always trustworthy, and would use the treaty to get land or money for their own families and less for the tribe. Another trick was that the natives were sometimes given too much whiskey before signing a treaty. The whiskey caused the natives to be careless, and they signed treaties without thinking. Finally, natives were moved to *reservations* in the West, which were areas of land that the U.S. government said would never be taken from them. Then the U.S. government took the land from the natives and moved them again!

For over 100 years afterwards, the Chicago portage area was an important location for fur trading. The Potawatomi knew the land and were expert **trappers.**[10] Traders traded all types of European goods like axes, fabric, knives, and muskets to the Potawatomi for pelts. The beaver became a unit of money between the European trader and the native. Two yards of red

---

[10] trappers = people who trap, kill, and remove the skin from animals

cloth would cost six beaver pelts, and an ax could be traded for two good beaver pelts.[11]

How did this little creek and this animal attract Europeans to Chicago?

Did you figure it out?

Collect one star if you answered that Portage Creek allowed boats to sail from France and Canada all the way to the Gulf of Mexico. This shortcut made it easier for French and Canadian fur traders to trade European goods for beaver and other pelts with the Potawatomi in Chicago. Since Lake Michigan and the Chicago River were so useful for transportation, a city grew where they met. The two blue stripes on the city flag represent the Chicago River and Lake Michigan.[12]

---

[11] Gilman, *Where Two Worlds Meet*

[12] Some sources state that the stripes represent the two branches of the Chicago River.

[FOLLOW THE FUR ON ITS JOURNEY!]

Learn how native groups used pelts to trade for goods. Then "sail" back to Canada to see how the fur was used to make fashionable goods.

Isle a la Cache Museum
501 E. Romeo Road
Romeoville, IL 60446-1538
(815) 886-1467
http://www.reconnectwithnature.org/visitor-centers/icm

[TRAVEL BACK IN TIME!]

Meet early settlers, traders, and natives at the annual Des Plaines Valley Rendezvous in Willow Springs, Illinois. Visit www.ariverthruhistory.com for schedule and information.

Wigwams at the Des Plaines Valley Rendezvous.

[**SEE WHAT LOUIS JOLLIET AND FATHER JACQUES MARQUETTE SAW.**]

Free walking tours are offered between May and November.

Chicago Portage National Historic Site.
Portage Woods Forest Preserve
4800 S. Harlem Avenue
Lyons, IL 60534
www.chicagoportage.org

Sculpture of Marquette and Jolliet in Portage Woods.

Investigation 3:

What can Chicago thank for its beginning?

Possible answers:
a) Beavers
b) A trading post
c) French fashion

Find clues in the illustration to help you answer the questions:

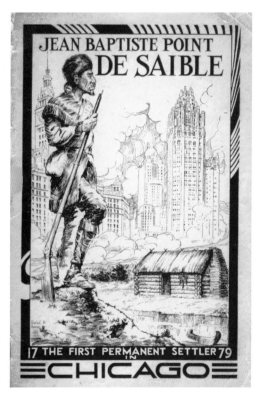

- Who is the man in the picture?
- In what year did he **settle**[1] in Chicago?
- From what type of material is his hat made?
- From what type of material are his clothes made?
- What special details can you find on his boots? What might their purpose be?
- What is he holding in his right hand?
- Why might he need this object?

Look at the details of the small building:

- From what materials is this building made?
- On the front of the building is an object that advertises this business to customers. What is it?
- For what purpose is the canoe used?
- Are the buildings in the background from the same time period as the building in the front? How can you tell?
- Why does the artist show both types of buildings?

Let's think about early Chicago. You've already learned that beavers and French fashion helped the Chicago area get noticed by European explorers. French explorers came to *Chicagou* (sometimes also

---

[1] settle = to make a place your home

Bronze sculpture of DuSable on Michigan Avenue near the Chicago River.

called *Chicagoua*, *Chikagou*, or *Eschikago*) and were happy to discover many animals, especially beavers, that could be killed and skinned to be used in fashionable French clothing.

One hundred years or so after the French had abandoned the area, the first **nonnative[2] settler[3]** moved into Chicagou. Jean Baptiste Point DuSable (sometimes spelled *de Saible* or *de Sable*) was born in

---

[2] nonnative = describing a person not born in the place where he or she lives

[3] settler = one who settles in a place

This sign marks the spot of the old trading post.

the Haitian city of Saint-Marc in 1745. DuSable was educated in France and loved European art. He spoke French, English, and Spanish, and he later learned several Indian languages as well. When he was about 20 years old (around 1765), he left Haiti for New Orleans. He was injured and lost his identity papers on the way when his boat sunk. Some priests hid DuSable while he recovered. He then avoided slavery in the South by moving north up the Mississippi River. He settled in Illinois, where he befriended and joined a Potawatomi tribe. There, DuSable married a Potawatomi woman, and they had two children, a boy and a girl.

By 1779, DuSable had moved with his family and started a successful **trading post**[4] in Chicago at the

---

[4] trading post = a station set up for trading goods

These buildings now stand near the site of DuSable's trading post.

mouth of the Chicago River. In this location, he constructed a log mansion which included a trading post, barns, a mill, a dairy, a bake house, and a smokehouse. DuSable's home was luxurious with fine furniture, a feather bed, and his European art collection.

The trading post was a booming business, trading all kinds of goods (including fur, bread, and meat) to native tribes, trappers, and other traders coming through the area. Because of DuSable's successful trading post, other settlers moved into the area. The success of DuSable's trading post created the very first settlement in Chicagou. For this reason, DuSable is known as the Father of Chicago. Thank you, DuSable!

What can Chicago thank for its beginning?

Did you figure it out?

Help yourself to one star if you inferred that a trading post was responsible for starting the first settlement in Chicago.

[VISIT THE SITE OF DUSABLE'S TRADING POST.]

DuSable's trading post is long gone, but you can visit the area where the trading post once stood on the north bank of the Chicago River near Michigan Avenue.

In October 2010, the Michigan Avenue Bridge was renamed DuSable Bridge to honor Chicago's founding father.

[SEE STONES FROM THE WORLD'S HISTORIC BUILDINGS.]

Tribune Tower has a cool collection of historic stones from all over the world embedded in the lower part of its outside walls.

Tribune Tower
435 N. Michigan Avenue
Chicago, IL 60611

Investigation 4:

What is the purpose of a fort?

First, you'll need to examine the different pieces that make up a fort. Find clues in the pictures to help you answer the questions:

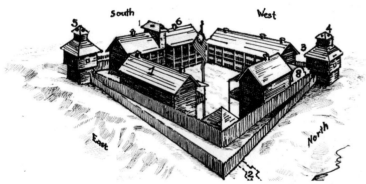

Fort Dearborn.

The replica of Old Fort Wayne in Fort Wayne, Indiana.

- How many fences surround the buildings? What purpose might they serve?
- Are the fences tall or short? What is their purpose?
- Do the buildings have windows? Why or why not?
- Who lives here? Do many or a few people live here?
- For what purpose might the center area be used?
- Of what material are the buildings made? Does the material look strong or weak? Why do you think this material was used?
- What body of water surrounds these buildings on the north and east?
- What country's flag flies above the buildings?
- What is the purpose of a fort? Why do you think so?

Read on to check your thinking.

Inside Old Fort Wayne, which has the same design as Fort Dearborn. Both forts were designed by Captain John Whistler.

By the late 1700s, the world began to notice the area that would one day become Chicago, which was then part of the Northwest Territory. The French, British, Americans, and the Potawatomi (who had already settled in the area) all wanted Chicago for themselves.

Between 1776 and 1783, American colonists had fought and won the Revolutionary War with England. In 1795, the colonists took control from the natives of the six square miles of land at the mouth of the Chicago River. Because it was such a valuable trading area with its connecting waterways, the United States ordered a **fort**[1] built there to protect the area from being taken by England. The fort would also protect the settlers from the surrounding native groups.

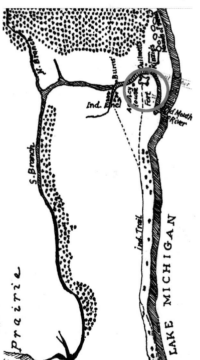

In July of 1803, the U.S. war secretary for President Thomas Jefferson, Henry Dearborn, ordered Captain John

---

[1] fort = a strong building where soldiers live to protect an area and to stay protected themselves

Whistler and 68 soldiers from Detroit, Michigan, to build a fort on the south bank of the Chicago River. The site of the fort was just across from DuSable's trading post, which John Kinzie owned beginning in 1804. Captain Whistler and his family sailed to Chicago by boat. In Chicago, the Whistler family joined the soldiers, who with Lieutenant James Swearingen, had marched from Detroit to the mouth of the Chicago River.

Captain Whistler designed the fort and, with his soldiers, built it of **timbers**[2] from nearby forests. Since the men had no horses or oxen to help, they hauled the trees by rope and floated them across the river to the site where the fort would be built. When Fort Dearborn was completed later that summer, it had two *blockhouses* at opposite corners (#4 and #5 in the drawing). Blockhouses were buildings made of heavy timbers with small openings used for defending the fort with gunfire. A secret, underground tunnel called a *sally-port* (#2) led from the fort to the river. During an attack, the tunnel could be used for hiding or for getting water without leaving the fort. Next to the blockhouse, the smaller semicircular building, the *magazine* (#8), held barrels of gunpowder used for the guns and three **cannons.**[3]

---

[2] timbers = wood from trees
[3] cannon = a large, heavy gun on a stand

The larger buildings were barracks where officers and soldiers lived. In the center was an open space used for the soldiers to line up before their officers, for doing chores, or as a gathering place. Surrounding the fort were two sets of *palisades*, which are fences made of heavy wooden stakes for extra protection.

Rebekah Wells Heald.

For many years, Fort Dearborn was a peaceful place. John Kinzie's trading post became the official trading post of the fort, supplying soldiers, settlers, and Potawatomi with goods they needed. Many Potawatomi were friendly with soldiers and settlers. Americans and Potawatomi competed in foot races against each other. Families like the Leighs and Kinzies had Potawatomi friends and shared meals together in the settlers' homes. The soldiers even tended their own garden outside the fort.

Captain Whistler left the fort in 1810, and Captain Nathan Heald took charge. A year later, Captain Heald married Rebekah Wells and brought her to Fort Dearborn to live. Feeling protected by the nearby fort, even more settlers moved into the area. Because Fort

Dearborn was so important for the growth of Chicago, it is represented by the first red star on the Chicago flag.

What is the purpose of a fort?

Did you figure it out?

Collect a star if you decided that a fort is used for protection.

This land is your land, this land is my land. Wait... Whose land is this anyway?

Over 10,000 years ago, the first immigrants came to North America on foot. They crossed the Bering Strait, which was a land bridge that connected Russia to Alaska.

These first immigrants, who we now call Native Americans, settled all across North America in communities. Each native group developed their own way of life, or *culture*. A group's culture includes its language, religion, entertainment, foods, and styles of clothing and housing. Each community also had their own forms of government and laws.

In the late 1600s, the French first explored native lands in the Northwest Territory (land now known as the states of Illinois, Indiana, Ohio, Wisconsin, and Michigan). French immigrants began to move into the Northwest Territory alongside native communities.

Then the British took notice of the territory and began fighting against the French and Indians in 1754 to take it. The British won the *French and Indian War* by 1763 and took ownership of the Northwest Territory.

Great Britain owed large amounts of money, called debts, after the French and Indian War ended. To pay off the debts, King George decided he would charge the British colonists living in North America extra money (a *tax*) on all paper goods. The colonists were angry and planned to separate from Great Britain. They wanted to start their own country. A little more than 100 years later, the colonists won their war for independence against Great Britain and started their own country called the United States.

By 1779, George Rogers Clark and a group of 175 Americans beat the British and captured the Northwest Territory for the United States.

Leaders of territories in the Northwest needed more people in order to become a new state. To bring more people to settle a territory, leaders offered free land to anyone who would come and build on it. Eventually American settlers outnumbered the native groups who had lived on the land for thousands of years. Living together changed the cultures of both groups.

American culture became a little more like natives' cultures than their old British culture. American settlers hunted, fished, and farmed like natives; learned native methods for building, cooking, and fighting; and added bits of native language to their own. The American style of dress started to look more like the natives' styles than British. Americans had to **adapt**[1] to their new home in the wilderness, and to do that they looked to the natives for ideas.

Native American culture changed greatly after the American settlers arrived. Americans over-hunted animals that natives depended on for food, clothing, weapons, tools, and shelter. Unable to hunt, natives started to rely on the American trading posts for food, clothing, and other goods. Natives started to add American clothing to their traditional outfits. Some natives became addicted to a European drink called whiskey, which sometimes caused them to get sick or die. European and American diseases killed many natives. Sometimes natives caught these diseases by accident, and other times Americans put germs on goods given to natives to make them sick. Ever since the first Europeans had arrived from France in 1673, natives were being taught to change their religion. Finally, the United States government forced the natives off of their homelands, pushing them farther and farther west.

Not all the native groups gave up their land without a fight. Great leaders like Tecumseh and Chief Black Hawk brought native tribes together to fight the Americans. They wanted to return to their old way of life and keep their land. However, these attempts failed and native groups eventually left the Chicago area and moved west.

So, *whose land is this anyway?*

---

[1] adapt = to make changes

FIND THE SITE OF FORT DEARBORN DOWNTOWN.

The intersection of Michigan Avenue and Wacker Drive.

Chicago Landmark plaque for Fort Dearborn.

Investigation 5:

What happened here? What led to it?

Find clues in the photograph to help you answer the questions:

- Observe the style of clothing and hair of each figure. From what cultural groups are they?
- Can you find men, women, and children?

- What are the different types of weapons in the sculpture?
- What lies at the feet of the men?
- Are the people sad, angry, fearful, excited? What do their facial expressions and actions show you?
- What does the figure above the people represent?
- Why did the artist decide to include this figure?

What do you think happened here? What causes led to it? Why do you think so?

On June 12, 1812, the United States declared war on Great Britain. Part of the reason for this war was that the United States hoped to keep the Northwest Territory, and also win Canada from Great Britain. However, Great Britain planned to keep Canada, and

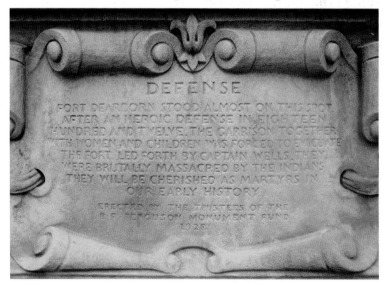

also take the Northwest Territory (including Chicago) away from the United States. A little more than two years later, the war ended with each country keeping the land it had to begin with and no more.

In the meantime, many natives of the Chicago area were growing angry with the Americans. Americans had taken away their land, had killed most of the animals that their tribes hunted, and were changing the **culture**[1] of the Native Americans. There had been scattered attacks by natives on local settlers, although many natives were still friendly. Settlers and soldiers around Fort Dearborn grew nervous.

Great Britain made some Native American groups an offer they didn't refuse[2]: Get rid of the Americans, and we will give you back your land. Armed with American **muskets**[3] and British weapons, the native groups began successful attacks on U.S. forts.

On August 9, 1812, Captain Nathan Heald received an order from his boss, General William Hull, to **evacuate**[4] Fort Dearborn for Fort Wayne in the Indiana Territory. American men, women,

---

[1] culture = the way a group lives, including their language, religion, food, and entertainment

[2] Tecumseh, the legendary Shawnee chief, was one leader who joined the British. He attracted many groups of natives to join him in a confederacy in Prophetstown in what is now Indiana.

[3] musket = an old type of heavy gun that took one bullet at a time

[4] evacuate = to leave a place

and children in and around the fort began busily preparing for their 200-mile journey. Captain Heald met with Potawatomi leaders and promised them all of the supplies and animals that the soldiers would leave behind in exchange for a safe journey. On August 14, Rebekah Heald's uncle, William Wells, arrived with a group of 30 members of the Miami tribe who would help escort the group safely to their destination.

Close native friends of the Americans, like Potawatomi Chief Black Partridge, warned the Americans that the Potawatomi were planning to attack them as they evacuated the fort. Chief Black

Partridge, William Wells, and John Kinzie were some of the men who warned Captain Heald to stay at the fort, rather than be attacked in the open with hardly any weapons. Captain Heald would not listen. Being a military man, the captain would strictly follow orders

to evacuate, no matter what other information he received, unless General Hull ordered him otherwise.

At 9 a.m. on Saturday, August 15, 1812, the soldiers, as promised, gave the Potawatomi access to the fort's stored goods. However, they partially broke their promise by dumping the gunpowder and whiskey into the river. The natives were upset by this because they could have used the gunpowder in their hunting. On horseback, Rebekah's uncle Captain William Wells took the lead, followed by half of his Miami escorts also on horseback. Next in line were the 12 volunteer militia men and their teenaged sons, armed with muskets. Those of the 55 soldiers who were healthy walked next. Afterwards came the supply wagons and wagons carrying women, children,

Rebekah Wells Heald and her Uncle Billy, Captain William Wells.

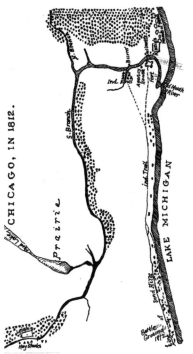

and sick and injured people. John Kinzie, his daughter Margaret Helm, and Rebekah Heald also rode on horseback. Last of all rode the rest of the Miami escorts. Kinzie's family sailed alongside the lakeshore by boat, having been warned that there was likely to be trouble.

Slowly, the group traveled south along the **sand dunes**[5] that lined the lakefront. About an hour and a half later, two miles south of Fort Dearborn, the 96 Americans were surprised by over 500 Potawatomi on horseback, armed with tomahawks, scalping knives, and muskets. Since it wasn't their fight, the Miami rode off, warning the Potawatomi that there would be payback for the attack on the evacuating Americans. After 15 minutes, Captain Heald **surrendered,**[6] ending the battle. Twenty-six soldiers (11 more were killed or died after surrendering), ten to twelve militia volunteers, two

[5] sand dunes = high ridges of sand formed by the wind
[6] surrender = to give up to the power of another

women (one more would die later), and an entire wagon of 12 children were **slaughtered**[7] and left lying along the sand dunes. Last, Fort Dearborn was burned to the ground by the Potawatomi. This battle became known as the Fort Dearborn **Massacre**[8].

Who survived and who died?

Rebekah Heald and her uncle William Wells both fought bravely. She survived, but her uncle did not. Rebekah's husband Captain Nathan Heald also survived. Later the Healds moved to Missouri and had a child. Captain Heald died two years after they moved.

Who survived and who died?		
	Total	Killed
U.S. Soldiers	55	37
Militia	12	12
Women	9	3
Children	18	13
Kinzie & Wells	2	1
Total Americans	96	66
Native Americans	about 500	15

Chief Black Partridge rescued the Kinzie family and all survived. Many American survivors were held as prisoners by the Potawatomi after the massacre, but were eventually released in exchange for money or goods. After the massacre, Americans stayed out of Chicago, too afraid

---

[7] slaughtered = killed in large numbers

[8] massacre = the killing of a large number of helpless or weak humans in a cruel way. The term *massacre* is offensive to some, so the Fort Dearborn Massacre is sometimes referred to at the Battle of Fort Dearborn.

of more attacks. Settlers began returning when the fort was rebuilt in 1816. By 1840, a fort was no longer needed. The Chicago area was no longer under attack by natives or other countries. It was torn down in 1857.

What happened here? What causes lead to it?

Did you figure it out?

Collect another star if you predicted that there had been a deadly battle.

[**EXPLORE ANOTHER FORT DESIGNED BY JOHN WHISTLER.**]

Fort Dearborn's soldiers and settlers never made it to Fort Wayne, but you can!

Historic Fort Wayne
1101 Spy Run Avenue
Fort Wayne, IN 46805
www.oldfortwayne.org

[VISIT THE MASSACRE SITE.]

What were once sand dunes later became Prairie Avenue, a street for Chicago's wealthiest residents like George Pullman, Marshall Field, and Charles Kimball. The 1800 and 1900 blocks of Prairie Avenue are now part of the historic Prairie Avenue District. Glessner House helps preserve and share the area's history.

Glessner House Museum
1800 S. Prairie Avenue
Chicago, IL 60616
(312) 326-1480
www.glessnerhouse.org

[REMEMBER THE VICTIMS OF THE 1812 MASSACRE.]

Battle of Fort Dearborn Park
E. 18th Street and S. Calumet Parkway
Chicago, IL 60616

Investigation 6
What caused Chicago to BOOM?

Once a decade, the United States government counts the *population* (number of people) of the country. This is called a *census*. *Deca-* means ten, and a decade has ten years. A census is taken every ten years.

Analyze the data for clues to help you answer the questions:

- Between which two consecutive decades do you see the largest population growth, or **boom**[1]?
- Which decade shows the second

Population of Chicago by Decades		
Year	Population	Percentage of growth
1830	100	
1840	4,470	4370%
1850	29,963	570%
1860	112,172	274%
1870	298,977	167%
1880	503,185	68%
1890	1,099,850	118%
1900	1,698,575	54%
1910	2,185,283	29%
1920	2,701,705	24%
1930	3,376,438	25%
1940	3,396,808	0.7%
1950	3,620,962	7%
1960	3,550,404	–2%
1970	3,369,357	–5%
1980	3,005,072	–11%
1990	2,783,726	–7%
2000	2,896,016	4%
2010	2,695,598	–6.9%

[1] boom = sudden population growth

48

Lock 6 in Channahon, Illinois.

largest percentage of population growth?

■ What are reasons that people move to a new place?

■ What caused so many people to come to Chicago?

It would have been exciting news for Louis Jolliet, if it had been announced 163 years earlier!

In 1836 the state of Illinois announced that a canal would be dug connecting Lake Michigan to the Illinois River. Hooray! This was exciting news for the people of Chicago and all of Illinois. Ninety-six miles of canal would be dug by hand from Chicago to connect the waters of the Illinois River and Lake Michigan. Shipping goods would be much faster by water, and boats that were too large to pass through the tiny Portage Creek could pass through the wider canal. The Illinois and

Michigan Canal (named for the two bodies of water it would connect) would bring money to the people of Illinois and make Chicago a very important **port.**[2]

With a big ceremony on July 4, 1836, work on the canal began in what is now the Bridgeport neighborhood in Chicago. **Immigrants,**[3] mainly from Ireland and Germany, left their home countries to earn money by digging the canal. As new immigrants arrived, more goods and services were needed. Some goods and services that canal workers and their families needed were food, clothing, banks, churches, and schools. More people came to start businesses to supply the needed goods and services to the growing population of Chicago. The population boomed between 1830 and 1840, growing larger than at any other time in the entire history of Chicago!

Canal workers used pickaxes to cut through limestone.

The work was hard and dangerous. Canal workers dug six feet deep and 60 feet wide through limestone. They used pickaxes, shovels, and *black powder* (gunpowder). If the

---

[2] port = a city or town where ships can load and unload goods
[3] immigrants = people who leave their home countries to live in a new country

stone was too hard to cut with a pickaxe, workers had to drill a hole, fill it with black powder, and light the black powder. Then they had to run for cover before the stone exploded into bits. Many workers died in black powder accidents. Workers were paid a dollar a day for their work, and were happy to have it. More and more people came for the jobs that would be created by the canal's existence.

A short time after the work had begun, it stopped. Why? 1837 was a hard year for the United States. Banks and businesses failed, and many people lost their land and homes. This time was called the Panic of 1837. Illinois could no longer afford to pay the canal workers. Canal leaders tried to keep work going by paying workers in *scrip*, which was paper that said that the canal would pay when it had money again. A few stores accepted the

Canal *scrip* was used to pay the workers when money ran out.

scrip from workers, but at a value of only 15 cents for every dollar. The only way scrip could be used for its full value was to buy land owned by the canal. Soon workers refused to work for scrip, and the digging stopped.

By 1843, Illinois still had no money to pay canal workers, but rich men from New York, England, and France paid nearly two million dollars to complete the canal. Work started again in March 1845. Yellow limestone was discovered when workers began digging again, and was sold as a building material. This special type of limestone was used for buildings like Chicago's Water Tower, and even for some private homes in the area. Limestone meant thousands more jobs for people, especially Irish immigrants, along the canal.

In April 1848, the canal finally opened, making Chicago one of the most important ports in the country! Before the canal opened, horses and mules had been used to transport farm crops to be sold. The animals couldn't carry too much weight and took a long time.

With the canal, goods like **lumber**[4] and huge amounts of harvested crops like wheat and corn could be shipped faster, farther, and more cheaply from farms in Illinois. Corn became cheaper to ship and made an enormous amount of money for farmers. Farmers started planting

---

[4] lumber = wood

Hogan Grain Elevator in Seneca, Illinois.

even more crops and hiring more people to help with the work of planting, harvesting, and shipping.

Towering grain elevators were built in the area for storing, weighing, and loading the grain onto boats. Giant warehouses were built to store goods along the canal. Chicago opened its Board of Trade in March 1848 to handle the extreme amounts of grain trading that were expected because of the canal. More and more people came for all of the jobs the canal made possible.

Paper and cardboard factories, steel and iron **plants,**[5] and meatpacking plants opened up all along the canal, making it easy to ship goods where they were needed. Goods from the south like sugar, molasses, salt, and oranges could be shipped to Chicago for the first time, thanks to the canal. Of course, people were needed to

---

[5] plants = factories that make one type of product

work in the factories and to help sell and ship the goods.

Thousands of passengers paid to travel along the canal on *packet boats* (so named because they transported packets of mail). Packet boats were attached by rope to horses that pulled

Chicago's Board of Trade at 141 W. Jackson Boulevard.

the boats along the canal. Travel by boat was so much faster and cleaner than having **oxen**[6] pull a wagon through mud and dust and camping outside along the way. A packet boat sped along the canal at a whopping five miles per hour!

Many workers were needed to operate the canal. Teams of mules that pulled the heavy freight boats by rope were led up and down the paths by young boys. Mules were cared for at mule barns and brought back and forth to the canal. Toll collectors collected money from boats using the canal. Workers were hired to

---

[6] oxen = male cattle used for farm work or heavy shores, similar to bulls

load and unload the grain and check, weigh, and store the grain. The boats had crews of workers too.

Because the water level was different in different parts of the canal, boats were *locked* in a space between two heavy wooden gates where the water level was raised or lowered by a *locktender*. Once the boat was at the right water level, the locktender cranked the gates open and the boat passed through. The locktender lived in a house next to the gates, and was on duty for 24 hours every day of the week.

Packet boats made travel faster and cleaner for passengers.

The Illinois and Michigan Canal brought a lot of people and money into the area. These people bought land, started businesses, and built communities in Chicago.

The heavy gates of the lock (above).
A locktender's house on the canal (below).

What caused Chicago to BOOM?

Did you figure it out?

Did you figure out that many people came to Chicago between 1830 and 1850 for a better life? Immigrants left their homes to find jobs and provide better lives for their families. When people came to Chicago, they built communities that offered the goods and services they would need. Collect a star if you were correct!

[CHECK OUT THE CANAL REGION.]

There are many interesting places to visit along the Illinois and Michigan Canal. You can see mule barns, warehouses, grain elevators, and even ride on a packet boat. Visit www.canalcor.org for more information.

[TAKE A WALKING TOUR AND VISIT THE MUSEUM.]

The Gaylord Building in Lockport, Illinois, is constructed from dolomite limestone from the canal.

Gaylord Building
200 W. 8th Street
Lockport, IL 60441
(815) 838-9400
www.gaylordbuilding.org

[CRUISE THE CANAL!]

Ride on a mule-pulled replica packet boat.

Lock 16 Visitor Center
754 First Street
LaSalle, IL
(815) 220-1848
http://lasallecanalboat.org

[VISIT AN ORIGINAL GRAIN ELEVATOR.]

Hogan Grain Elevtor is an original grain elevator on the canal.

Hogan Grain Elevator
124 W. Williams
Seneca, IL 61360
(815) 357-6197
http://www.dnr.illinois.gov/
  recreation/greenwaysandtrails/
  Pages/IMCanal.aspx

[VISIT THE CLARKE HOUSE.
IT'S OLDER THAN THE CITY ITSELF!]

It's older than the city of Chicago! Henry Brown Clarke was a New Yorker who had heard about the promising settlement on the shores of Lake Michigan. In June 1835, Mr. Clarke bought 20 acres of land along the south shore of Lake Michigan for $10,000. There, among the prairies and Potawatomi camps, he built a home and raised a family. Mr. Clarke did very well, even becoming the director of the city's first bank, the Illinois State Bank. After the bank failed during the hard times of 1837, the Clarkes began farming and hunting to make money. Mrs. Clarke sold all but three of the original 20 acres after her husband died of cholera in 1849. The Clarke land added four blocks of homes to the growing city of Chicago.

Clarke House
1827 S. Indiana Ave.
Chicago, IL 60616
(312) 326-1480
www.clarkehousemuseum.org

The Clarke House was built before Chicago was a city. Some of the Clarkes' land was sold to the growing city of Chicago.

Investigation 7
What happened on March 4, 1837?

Find clues in the photographs to help you answer the questions:

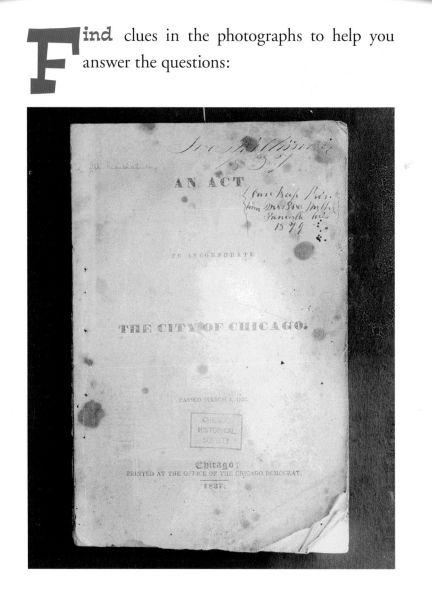

- What words and dates are alike in both photographs?
- What is an act?
- What kinds of things get *passed*?
- Have you ever seen the symbol before? Where?

Think about what the figures in the circle mean:

- Who does the Native American on the grass represent?
- What does the striped shield remind you of?
- What people are in the ship sailing toward the natives' land?
- What does the baby in the oyster shell mean? What is usually found inside an oyster?

■ How do all of these ideas relate to Chicago?

The 350 settlers living in Chicago decided that they needed to organize their community with government leaders and laws. The settlers asked the State of Illinois for a town **charter**,[1] which created a group of elected leaders called the Board of Trustees. Chicago was made an official town on August 12, 1833. Little Chicago was almost a half square mile in size, and had Kinzie, Desplaines, Madison, and State Streets as its boundaries. But by 1836, the little town grew to 4,170 **residents**[2] who needed more order and more powerful leaders.

On March 4, 1837, the city of Chicago was born! Chicago received its first city charter, which is a legal paper from the state government making Chicago a city with a local government. The charter stated that the city would be *governed*, or led, by an **elected**[3] mayor and other leaders. The city of Chicago held its first mayoral election on May 2, 1837, and elected William B. Ogden as its first mayor. The mayor is the top leader in Chicago. The mayor gives directions to other city departments and hires department leaders like the chief of police, fire chief, and school superintendent.

---

[1] charter = a legal document that creates a town or city
[2] residents = people who reside, or live, in a place
[3] elected = chosen by voting

The city is divided into smaller sections called wards. The people in each ward are represented by an alderman in decision-making meetings with the mayor.

The mayor also passes or **vetoes**[4] **ordinances**[5] from the city council. The mayor is elected for a four-year term.

The charter also divided the city into smaller **wards,**[6] each with its own boss called an alderman. What started out in 1837 as six wards reached 50 wards by 2012. About once a month, the mayor and aldermen hold a **city council**[7] meeting at City Hall to discuss problems, make ordinances for the city, and decide how to spend **tax**[8] money. Your alderman represents

---

[4] veto = to officially turn down an idea so it doesn't become a law
[5] ordinances = rules that must be followed
[6] wards = areas of a city, divided up for voting and decision-making
[7] city council = a group of people who makes laws for a city
[8] tax = money paid to the government that is used for public purposes

your wants and needs in these meetings because if she or he doesn't, you won't vote for her or him again.

So, what does the symbol mean? It is the official seal of Chicago, designed on March 4, 1837, when Chicago was officially made a city. The red, white, and blue shield in the center shows that Chicago supports the United States of America. The idea of *plenty*, or having enough, is represented by the bundle of wheat (a crop grown in the area). The Native American represents the groups such as the Potawatomi who lived here before any explorers arrived. The sailing ship shows that people came from across the seas to establish new communities and businesses. The baby in the shell shows that Chicago is a *pearl*, a city of great value. *Urbs in Horto* is Chicago's **motto,**[9] and it means "city in a garden" in Latin.

What happened on March 4, 1837?

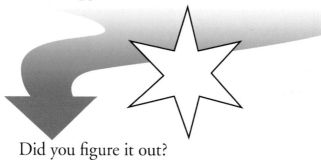

Did you figure it out?

---

[9] motto = a saying that shows the personality of a person, place, or thing

Collect a star if you figured out that March 4, 1837, was Chicago's birthday!

[**OBSERVE THE MEETINGS OF OUR LOCAL GOVERNMENT.**]

The mayor and city council meet at City Hall to discuss and vote on the **budget,**[10] traffic control, city planning, and more. View the Chicago City Council calendar at: www.chicityclerk.com Find a ward alderman at: www.cityofchicago.org.

City Hall (a Chicago Landmark)
121 N. LaSalle Street, 2nd floor
Chicago, IL 60602

City Hall, inside (left) and out (right).

---

[10] budget = a document that says how money should be spent

[Govern your own city!]

At Journey World, kids are responsible for government, public safety, operating successful businesses, and providing goods and services to the citizens of their city. Children from ages 5 to 17 are welcome to visit in groups of 25 to 125.

Visit http://www.girlscoutsgcnwi.org/ and search for "journey world" to check it out.

Journey World
770 N. Halstead Street
Chicago, IL 60642
(312) 912-6371

Investigation 8:

Missing: Chicago's Downtown. Where did it go?

Figure out what happened to this toy, and you'll figure out what destroyed Chicago's downtown.

Find clues in the photograph to help you answer the questions:

- What shapes and colors do you see?
- The toy is made of glass. Glass melts at 2,597°F to 2,930°F (1425°C to 1600°C). Could this have been done by a child? Why or why not?
- What type of toy do you think this was?
- What do you think caused it to look like this?

With faster transportation and more jobs, swarms of people continued to move into Chicago. People were settling in the city quickly and they needed places to live—fast!

A Chicago carpenter found a way to build homes easily, cheaply, and quickly. In 1833 he built St. Mary's Church for only $400, using wooden boards and unskilled workers. Other **architects**[1] didn't like this cheap way of building. They called it *balloon-frame* construction because they said the building was so light it would blow away like a balloon. However,

This model shows balloon-frame construction.

---

[1] architect = a person who designs buildings

this was exactly the type of fast construction that Chicago needed. Not only was balloon-framing quick, but it was easy enough for just two people to do. Plus, wood was easy to get since Chicago had become the largest lumber market in the country.

By 1871, the population of Chicago had grown to 334,270 people. Not only were 45,000 wooden buildings and homes crowded tightly in the city, hundreds of miles of streets and sidewalks were wooden as well. Even fancy buildings like Field and Leiter's Department Store, the Palmer House Hotel, and the mansions of wealthy people were constructed of wood, with marble or stone exteriors.

Being built mainly of wood, the city of Chicago had had many fires. After a fire killed 23 people in 1857, trained firefighters took over the work of the **volunteer**[2] fire department. The fire department had new fire engines and ladders,

This call box, which stands on Michigan Avenue today, is similar to the call boxes used in 1871.

[2] volunteer = a person who chooses to do a service without being paid

Making Chicago: Checking in on our Growing City

The picture at the top shows a view of the city from the water works in 1870. Can you find grain elevators, factories, and homes? At this time, Chicago was mostly constructed of wood. Even buildings that were stone or brick on the outside were wood underneath. The streets and sidewalks were also built of wood.

The picture on the bottom is a scene at the mouth of the Chicago River. What types of buildings can you find in this picture?

but it only had 185 firefighters to protect a city of over 330,000 people. In 1865, almost 200 call boxes were placed around the city for residents to send an alarm to the fire station. Chicago's first courthouse kept a watchman looking out from its tower for fires. Once the watchman reported a fire, he would ring an 11,000-pound bronze bell to warn the city of danger.

Bronze plaque at City Hall showing the 1853 courthouse. The watchman would patrol around the cupola, the rounded dome at the top.

Some of the new buildings like Field and Leiter's Department Store, the courthouse, and the Palmer House Hotel claimed their buildings were fireproof. A new water tower and pumping station had been finished in 1869 to supply water for the city. Built of limestone, these structures were also considered safe from fires.

Just like today, the Chicago summers were hot back then. During the summer of 1871, Chicago was suffering through a **drought**.[3] With plenty of heat and no rain, the wooden city of Chicago was as dry as a matchstick. Because of the businesses located there (saw mills, grain elevators, stables filled with hay and wood shavings), one area had so many fires that firefighters nicknamed it *Red Flash*.

What types of items are highly flammable (burn quickly and easily)?	
wood?	grain?
hay?	water?
gas?	grease?

The Red Flash area lost four blocks to a fire on Saturday night, October 7, 1871. Firefighters worked through the night into Sunday afternoon, for 18 hours total, before the fire was finally put out. Some fire trucks, engines, and hoses were damaged in this fire, and the firefighters needed to rest and heal after their long night spent battling the hot blaze. Unfortunately they didn't get the rest they needed.

The very same night, Sunday, October 8, 1871, another fire was reported by residents of a West Side neighborhood from their bright red call box. The O'Learys' barn was burning at 137 DeKoven Street!

---

[3] drought = a long, dry time when there is no rain

The O'Leary cottage at 137 DeKoven Street was untouched by fire because the fire moved north from the barn.

The alarm never reached the courthouse.

Luckily nearby firefighters saw the fire and sped to DeKoven Street on their own. Already the fire had grown too large for one team of firefighters to handle. The watchman saw the flames from his tower on the courthouse and gave the operator the location and the order, "Send more firefighters!" Shortly afterwards, he realized he had sent the firefighters in the wrong direction! The fire grew larger.

Led quickly through the city by trails of factories and businesses producing highly burnable goods, the fire grew larger and hotter. Just imagine the fire burning through stables filled with dry hay and wood shavings, gas works, explosive grain elevators, saw

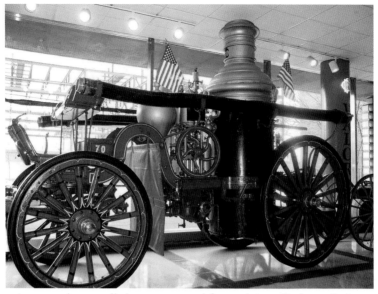

A *steamer,* horse-pulled steam-powered fire engine on display at Quinn Fire Academy.

mills, and lumber yards! Fire tornadoes whirled and fiery hot cinders rained on crowds of people running for their lives. Fleeing people carried all that they could save from their burning homes. Fiery sparks whipped across the Chicago River by the high howling wind starting new fires where they landed. The greasy surface of the polluted Chicago River even caught fire! Crowds of people ran, some safely reaching the waters of Lake Michigan and the wide open Potters' Field cemetery of Lincoln Park.

The watchman rang the bronze bell for five hours, warning the city until the courthouse itself caught on fire. Nonviolent prisoners were released from the

This fire engine was pulled by firefighters, according to the firefighters at Quinn Fire Academy in Chicago.

courthouse cells and others were taken away. The 11,000-pound bronze bell finally crashed through the courthouse floors as fire devoured the building.

The wooden roof of the new pumping station even caught fire and collapsed on the pumping machinery. No more water would be pumped to put out the flames.

What started around 9:00 p.m. on Sunday, October 8, raged for almost 30 hours, destroying the entire downtown area of Chicago. Finally, early on the morning of Tuesday, October 10, the drought ended. Rain fell, putting out the flaming city.

Chicago had burned from Taylor Street on the south to Fullerton Avenue on the north, three and one-half square miles of destruction. Fire destroyed 17,450

The St. James Hotel after the fire.

buildings including the *fireproof* Field & Leiter's, the Palmer House Hotel, the Tribune building, and the courthouse. Only the limestone Water Tower and Pumping Station survived. So did the wooden frame house of Mahlon Ogden, which stood alone at Clark and Oak Streets (now the site of the Newberry Library). Chicago lost around 300 residents, and 90,000 were left homeless. The fire had caused $200 million in damages to the city. The O'Learys' cottage, which was south of the barn, stood untouched by flames. The cause of the Great Chicago Fire is still unknown. Mrs. O'Leary was found not guilty of starting the fire by the Board of Police and Fire Commissioners in December

1871, and again by the Chicago City Council in 1997.

Missing: Chicago's Downtown. Where did it go?

Did you figure it out?

Collect a star if you answered correctly. Chicago's downtown area was almost completely destroyed by a huge fire. These glass marbles were discovered melted together after the Great Fire. The Great Fire of 1871 is remembered by the second star on Chicago's flag.

What caused the Great Chicago Fire?

To this day, nobody knows for sure. Some historians believe that Daniel "Pegleg" Sullivan, who was first to spot the fire, may have started it while taking milk from the O'Learys' dairy cow. Sullivan testified at the O'Leary trial that he ran (with a wooden leg) almost 200 feet to put out the fire and rescue the animals from the barn. There was a house blocking the view of the barn, however, from the location he claimed to have seen the fire. The commissioners never checked into Pegleg's story.

[STAND WHERE THE GREAT CHICAGO FIRE OF 1871 STARTED.]

The Robert J. Quinn Fire Academy now stands on the site where the Great Fire began. A sculpture, *Pillar of Fire*, out front marks the historic event. Inside visitors can see steam-powered and horse-drawn fire engines, a memorial to fallen firefighters, and a plaque marking the spot of the O'Leary cottage.

Quinn Fire Academy
558 W. DeKoven Street
Chicago, IL 60607
(312) 747-7239

[VISIT THE SURVIVORS.]

Stop by the only public buildings to survive in the area destroyed by the Fire of 1871, the Chicago Water Tower and Pumping Station. The City Gallery inside the historic water tower is a free gallery displaying the photography and art of local artists.

Chicago Water Tower
806 N. Michigan Avenue
Chicago, IL 60611

The limestone Water Tower was
designed by W.W. Boyington, 1869.

Across the street from the Water Tower, the historic
pumping station is now home to the Water Works
Visitor Center. Chicagoans and tourists can visit to
learn all about exploring Chicago and the many things
to do here.

Chicago Pumping Station
821 N. Michigan Avenue
Chicago, IL 60611
(312) 744-8783
www.explorechicago.org

The Pumping Station.

Investigation 9:

What effect did the Great Fire have on the spirit of Chicagoans?

Examine the sculptural relief for clues that tell how Chicagoans felt after the fire. Find clues in the photograph to help you answer the questions:

- Which figure represents the city of Chicago? Why do you think so?
- What is the female figure standing on? What do you think it represents? Why do you think so?
- Look closely at the expression and posture of each figure. How would you describe the attitude of the main figures? What do you think it means?
- What is in the background of the figures?
- What is each figure doing?
- What type of clothing is each figure wearing, and for what reason?
- What tools can you find? What are they used for?
- What does *regeneration* mean? The prefix *re-* means to do again. The base word *generate* means to create.

REGENERATION

THE GREAT CHICAGO FIRE IN OCTOBER EIGHTEEN HUNDRED AND SEVENTY-ONE DEVASTATED THE CITY FROM ITS ASHES THE PEOPLE OF CHICAGO CAUSED A NEW AND GREATER CITY TO RISE, IMBUED WITH THAT INDOMITABLE SPIRIT AND ENERGY BY WHICH THEY HAVE EVER BEEN GUIDED

ERECTED BY THE TRUSTEES OF THE B.F. FERGUSON MONUMENT FUND 1928

Regeneration at Michigan Avenue and Wacker Drive.

While the ashes of the city were still hot, *Chicago Tribune* owner (and soon to be mayor) Joseph Medill published a cheerful message to inspire the people of Chicago.

On October 11, 1871, Joseph Medill, owner of the *Chicago Tribune* wrote,

"CHEER UP ... the people of this once beautiful city have resolved that CHICAGO SHALL RISE AGAIN."

Chicagoans weren't ready to give up; they saw the fire as a chance to start anew and make an even better Chicago. No sooner did the ashes cool when the first load of wood for temporary housing was delivered. People who had fled the city returned and joined those who stayed to help rebuild Chicago. The remains of the downtown homes and buildings, rubble and ash, were swept into Lake Michigan to create more land along the lakefront. Marshall Field opened a temporary store in a barn. Potter and Bertha Palmer began making plans for a new Palmer House Hotel the very next day after the fire.

Mayor Roswell Mason issued **proclamations**[1] to keep Chicago's residents safe while the city was rebuilt. One proclamation was that bread had to be sold for

---

[1] proclamation = a public announcement

eight cents per loaf. Demand for bread would be high among the people who had lost everything in the fire, and the mayor did not want them to be overcharged. Some other proclamations made it illegal to smoke in the city and ordered people to be off the streets by a certain time at night (a *curfew*). A special police force of citizens was created to make sure these proclamations were being followed. Later the U.S. military took over.

Everybody wanted to help Chicago. A Relief and Aid Society was created to provide money, food, and temporary shelter to families left homeless by the blazing fire. Citizens of England, including Queen

An old water tank was used as a library after the fire.

Victoria, donated over 8,000 books to Chicago for a library. Because of this book donation, Chicago would set up its first public library. Until a permanent structure could be built, a temporary library was set up in an old water tank next to the temporary city hall.

In November 1871, Joseph Medill won the mayoral election and created strict *building codes* for a safer Chicago. Building codes are sets of safety laws about how buildings have to be constructed. Flammable building materials like wood were forbidden in the downtown area.[2]

Young architects, excited about rebuilding Chicago, arrived to try new building ideas. Land in the **Loop**[3] (Chicago's downtown area) would be very valuable, and architects did not want to waste space by building low buildings. Since an American inventor named Elisha Otis had designed the first steam-powered elevator in 1861, taller buildings became possible. The Chicago architects wanted to build *very* tall buildings. Louis Sullivan and his partner Dankmar Adler designed the Auditorium Building in 1889 with a foundation that floated on the marshy land like a giant raft. In 1881,

---

[2] Some residents argued that this law only allowed rich people to build downtown since regular and poor people couldn't afford nonflammable building materials.

[3] The Loop earned its nickname because of the circular route of the cable cars that operated around the business area.

architects Daniel Burnham and John Root designed a ten-floor, 130-foot-tall building named the Montauk Block.

Louis Sullivan and his partner Dankmar Adler designed the Auditorium Building in 1889, with a foundation that floated on the marshy land like a giant raft.

Steel, a new type of metal invented in 1855, was lightweight and strong and could be used to safely construct buildings so tall that they appeared to scrape the sky. William LeBaron Jenney designed the world's first *skyscraper* in Chicago (180 feet tall with 12 floors) with an iron and steel **skeleton**[4] for the Home Insurance Company in 1884. More and more skyscrapers grew from the city. With more office space available, more

---

[4] skeleton = a building's support inside the walls and floors

businesses moved into the Loop, making Chicago one of the largest cities in the United States.

Architects continue to bring their new designs to Chicago's skyscrapers. Today there are 1,105 skyscrapers towering over the Loop, with 100 more on the way. Built in 1974, the tallest skyscraper in Chicago is Willis Tower (better known as the Sears Tower). Willis Tower has 108 floors and is over 1,450 feet (442.14 meters) tall.

What effect did the Great Fire have on the spirit of Chicagoans?

Did you figure it out?

The people who stayed in Chicago felt determined and proud that they would rebuild their city even better and safer than before. Of course it was a tragedy for those who lost everything in the fire and for those who died. Without the Great Fire though, the Loop might still be a jumble of unsafe wooden buildings,

The city skyline from Soldier Field.

stables, grain elevators, lumberyards, and shacks. The fire brought people together who proudly rebuilt the city. A free public library was started with donated books from England. Parks and museums were built on land created by dumping rubble from the fire into Lake Michigan. Architects designed new types of buildings called skyscrapers. Without the fire, would Chicago be the beautiful architectural and cultural jewel on the lake that it is today?

Collect a star if you answered that Chicagoans felt the fire gave them a chance to build an even better city!

[MARVEL AT THE ADLER AND SULLIVAN MASTERPIECE.]

Auditorium Building
50 E. Congress Parkway
Chicago, IL 60605
(312) 922-2110
http://auditoriumtheatre.org

[TOUR CHICAGO BY BOAT, BUS, OR FOOT.]

The Chicago Architecture Foundation is located in the Sante Fe Building, which was designed by Daniel Burnham.

Chicago Architecture
    Foundation
224 S. Michigan Avenue
Chicago, IL 60604
(312) 922-3432, x240
www.architecture.org

Investigation 10:

What problems did immigrants face in their new homes?

Find clues in the cartoon to help you answer the questions:

This cartoon by artist Frank Beard was featured in the April 25, 1896, edition of *The Ram's Horn*, a Christian magazine published in Chicago by Frederick L. Chapman.

- What is the building behind the two characters?
- What are some symbols of the United States in the cartoon?
- What is Uncle Sam doing with his right hand? What does it mean?
- Look at each character's facial expression. How is each character feeling?
- How is the writing on the gate different from Uncle Sam's gesture and expression?
- Why is the immigrant labeled with the words **Sabbath desecration,**[1] **poverty,**[2] disease, **superstition,**[3] and **anarchy?**[4]
- Observe the immigrant's clothing, shoes, and hat. With his baggage, he carries books, a barrel, and a glass mug. What does the immigrant's appearance show about people's feelings towards immigrants at this time?
- Read the caption. Do Uncle Sam's words show that the United States wants the immigrant to come in, or not? Why do you think so?
- Do you think the artist agreed with negative

---

[1] Sabbath desecration = destroying the holy day (Sunday)

[2] poverty = being poor

[3] superstition = a belief that comes from not knowing better, a trust in magic

[4] anarchy = not having a government; for some this means complete freedom, for others complete chaos

feelings towards immigrants, or was he trying to show that these feelings were wrong? Why do you think so?

Who came to Chicago to live? The table below shows where immigrants came from, when they arrived in Chicago, and in which *decades* (ten year periods) they arrived.

Decades	Immigrants to Chicago	How many?
Before 1840	Germans, Irish, Norwegians	12,256
1840–1849	Irish, Germans	15,682
1850–1859	Germans, Irish	54,624
1860–1869	Germans, Irish, Bohemians, English	144,557
1870–1879	Germans, Swedes, Bohemians, Canadians	204,859
1880–1889	Germans, Swedes, Irish, Poles, Norwegians	450,666
1890–1899	Poles, Russians, Dutch, Italians, Bohemians	587,112
1900–1909	Russians, Austrians, Poles, Italians, Hungarians	783,428
1910–1919	Italians, Poles, Czechs	808,558
1920–1929	Italians, Poles, Lithuanians, Mexicans	859,409

Why did immigrants come to Chicago? In their native countries there may have been war, lack of food, unfair laws, or a lack of jobs. People left their homes and moved to Chicago for better opportunities. Immigrants may have been poor in their home countries. There were many jobs available in Chicago, and even unskilled workers could find work. Immigrants wanted to give their children a better life. In America, they could receive a better education and medical care, find better jobs, and have a chance for other life improvements.

New immigrants were faced with many problems upon their arrival to the city. Not being able to speak English made it more difficult to survive in their new home. Because the immigrants couldn't communicate with the residents, it made finding work and shelter, attending school, and other normal daily activities complicated. A hungry immigrant wouldn't be able to buy his or her favorite foods. Entertainment enjoyed in the home country wasn't available. Clothing the immigrants were used to wearing couldn't be found. Everything was new and different, and there was usually no help for the immigrants.

To feel more comfortable, immigrants from the same home countries gathered in neighborhoods together. The immigrants could then chat in their native language, buy the types of goods they enjoyed in the home country, and worship in their own religious buildings. These types of neighborhoods were known as *ethnic* neighborhoods. Many still exist in Chicago today, including neighborhoods for newer immigrant groups.

Arriving with little or no money, the new immigrants needed to find cheap shelter. Many immigrants in Chicago moved into crowded buildings called *tenements*. Tenements were buildings where several families would live in separate areas made up of a few tiny rooms. Usually these buildings were crowded with people and had no fresh air or indoor plumbing. They were located near factories or slaughterhouses. Immigrant adults

Ethnic neighborhoods help immigrants adjust to a new country.

Many immigrants lived in crowded, dirty tenements. This is an alley on the Near West Side in the 1920s or 30s.

and children would walk through dusty dirt roads at all hours of the day and night going to and from work. Very young children did *home work*, like pulling out stitching from clothes or sewing, to help their families make money. Crowded, dirty, and without indoor water and bathrooms, tenement conditions made it easy for diseases to spread throughout the neighborhoods.

Many Chicagoans felt that these new immigrant groups caused problems. The ethnic neighborhoods were thought to be dirty and a source of disease and crime. These Chicagoans accused new immigrants of being poor, dirty, and ignorant with strange beliefs. Some people complained that immigrants drank alcohol on Sundays, which most residents believed should be a day for worship, not for drinking alcohol.

Problems need solutions, and people tried to solve the "immigrant problem" in different ways. Neighborhood church schools taught upper-class American **customs**[5] to the immigrant children. Young boys were taught that gentlemen should stand when a lady enters the room, for example. English and personal cleanliness were taught at church schools.

Jane Addams was a **social activist**[6] who wanted to help the immigrants. Chicago's worst neighborhood in the late 1800s was on the West Side, which included the O'Leary house where the Great Fire began in 1871. The immigrants who lived there (mainly Italians, Bohemians, Germans, and Russians) faced the highest crime rate, the worst schools, and the worst housing in the city of Chicago. In 1889, Jane Addams leased the large brick home of Charles J. Hull at Polk and Halsted Streets and started a *settlement house*. A settlement house is a place that provides services to the public.

By living alongside the poor immigrants, Addams felt she would be able to better understand their problems. Free services offered to neighborhood residents at Hull-House included English and other classes for adults in the evenings, a nursery to care for babies while their mothers worked, a kindergarten, and clubs for older children. Hull-House gave the

---

[5] custom = the way a certain group of people behave, an unwritten rule
[6] social activist = a person who works to improve living conditions for a group of people

Hull-House was Jane Addams's solution to the "immigrant problem."

residents a place to bathe, a gym, a swimming pool, and the first public playground in Chicago. Addams hoped that by offering these free services and classes, she could improve the lives of the immigrants.

Hull-House received over 9,000 visitors per week to its programs, classes, and lectures. Not only did Addams use Hull-House to improve life for the West Side residents, but in 1895 she also improved the neighborhood. Rotting garbage in the alleys was piling up and spreading disease. Addams was appointed Garbage Inspector by the city. As inspector, Jane Addams followed the city garbage collectors through the neighborhood, making sure that they shoveled out all the garbage from the wooden garbage boxes. The neighborhood became cleaner and experienced less disease.

Hull-House helped get laws passed to protect women

and children. Some of the laws made workplaces safer, helped female and child workers to be treated better, and created a separate court system for children.

By 1908, Hull-House had added 13 buildings to the original house. It offered even more programs and services to the new immigrant groups in the neighborhood, which now included a large Greek population. Between 1930 and 1940, Mexican immigrants arrived to work in factories and railroads in the area. Hull-House was there to help these people adjust to their new home just as it had been for over 40 years. In 1931, Jane Addams was the first woman to receive the Nobel Peace Prize[7] for helping improve people's lives.

Immigrants still flock to Chicago for better opportunities, but the countries from which they come have changed. The 2010 census showed that the largest immigrant population in Chicago was from Mexico (41%). Polish immigrants were the next largest group (9%). The third largest group was from India (6%), with immigrants from the Philippines just behind them (5%). Since 1967, the Hull-House Museum, which includes two original Hull-House buildings, has been open to visitors on the University of Illinois at Chicago campus. The Hull-House Association

---

[7] Jane Addams shared the Nobel Prize with Nicholas Murray Butler.

remained in operation until early 2012 when it closed for financial reasons. It had continued Jane Addams's original purpose by offering classes for adults and children, providing job training, and trying to get laws changed to improve life for residents in need. However, because of lack of money, new immigrants to Chicago no longer have Hull-House classes and programs to help them adjust to their new country.

What problems did immigrants face in their new homes?

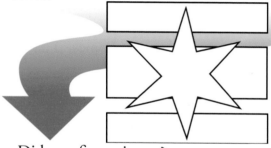

Did you figure it out?

Collect a star if you figured out what kinds of problems immigrants had to overcome in their new home.

While they struggled to make a better life in America, immigrants were treated unfairly by bosses, other residents, and even other immigrant groups. Life was difficult in a new country, and immigrants had little help adjusting to it. Many immigrants were poor, lived in overcrowded slums, and worked long hours for very little pay. Jane Addams was one Chicagoan who tried to help improve life for them.

Some of the people living in Chicago (and the rest of the United States) felt the immigrants were a problem. Immigrants were sometimes looked upon as dirty, ignorant, and poor. A portion of U.S. citizens blamed immigrants for causing problems for business owners, spreading disease, and causing crime.

The three white stripes of the Chicago flag represent the areas of the city where people live. The largest white stripe in the middle stands for the West Side, where early immigrants made their homes. The two narrow stripes on the top and bottom symbolize the North and South Sides of Chicago. The East Side, of course, is Lake Michigan.

[**VISIT THE HULL-HOUSE MUSEUM.**]

This is the original Hull-House built by Charles J. Hull in 1856. It stands on the campus of the University of Illinois at Chicago.

Hull-House Museum
800 S. Halsted Street
Chicago, IL 60607
(312) 413-5353
www.uic.edu/jaddams/hull

Investigation 11:

How was this town supposed to solve immigrant and labor problems?

Look at the map on the next page for clues to help you answer the questions:

- What is the name of this town?
- What was the population like in Chicago around the time of this map?
- What kinds of jobs did immigrants have around this time?
- What do the long dotted lines represent? Notice where these lines lead.
- Look at the names of the shops located in the center of the town. Can you figure out what is made here?
- Can you locate other places on the map? Find a school, an arcade, a playground, a hotel, a pump house, a gas works, a **brick yard,**[1] an ice house, and a **foundry.**[2]
- Where do people live, work, and play in this town?

---

[1] brick yard = a place where bricks are made from clay for building
[2] foundry = a place where metal is melted and made into different items

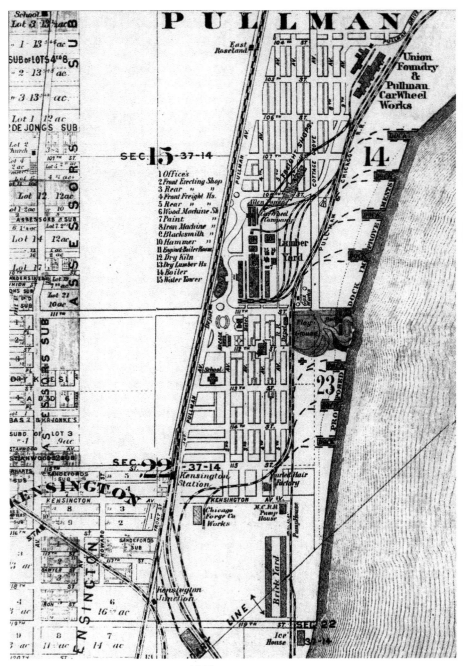

1885 map.

The Curled Hair Factory was a corporation started by Pullman residents in 1884. This business cleaned and processed Spanish moss from Louisiana to be used as stuffing for mattresses and furniture cushion padding. The company eventually went out of business because it couldn't compete with horse hair as a stuffing material.

The first automobile factory in the United States was started in 1893 by brothers Frank and Charles Duryea. What other types of transportation have wheels?

Right about the time that the Illinois and Michigan Canal was completed, the first train left from Chicago. Chicago's first mayor, William B. Ogden, believed that the future of transportation would be railroads. On October 25, 1848, Mayor Ogden, along with some important Chicagoans, reporters, farm goods, and supplies, was pulled along the tracks by a 12-year-old wood-burning locomotive called The Pioneer on the Galena and Chicago Union Railroad. Once the train reached its destination, in what is now Oak Park, Illinois, workers continued building tracks further west. Only 12 years later, Chicago had ten railroads and 4,000 miles of railroad track. By 1860, Chicago had become the major railroad center of the United States!

George Pullman, who had come from New York in 1857 to raise city buildings out of the mud, took an overnight train ride in New York. Unable to sleep on the uncomfortable train, Pullman spent the night thinking of a design for a comfortable sleeping car. Three years later Pullman had made enough money to create his first railroad sleeping car. Like Mayor Ogden, George Pullman saw that the future of transportation would be in railroads. He felt that people would pay more money to travel in comfort.

The Pioneer, Pullman's first sleeping car.

In 1865, Pullman finished building the sleeping car of his dreams, the Pioneer (not the locomotive of the same name). The Pioneer had red carpeting, hand-carved woodwork, and silver-trimmed coal lamps. Unfortunately, it seemed that the Pioneer would be a failure. The train car was too wide and too tall to pass through bridges and platforms on the railways. But in April of that year, President Abraham Lincoln was assassinated, and his body was brought by train from Washington, D.C., to his hometown of

Springfield, Illinois. Crowds gathered at every railroad crossing along the way to pay their respects to the dead president. As the train cars passed by, the country also got a look at Pullman's Pioneer sleeping car, carrying the Lincoln family home in comfort. The tragedy turned out to be great publicity for Pullman.

Pullman porter.

At age 36 in February 1867, George Pullman started his Pullman Palace Car Company in Chicago. His Palace Cars were like moving hotels with fancy food, dining cars, chandeliers, electric lighting, leather seats, silk lamp shades, heating, and air conditioning. To entertain and serve Palace Car guests, African-Americans, primarily migrants from the South, were hired as porters. These porters made sure the guests had everything they needed. They even entertained guests during their ride.

As time passed, workers in Chicago became angry over long hours working in unsafe areas for very little

Inside a Pullman Palace Car.

pay. Some of these laborers—men, women, and even children—began to **strike**[3] for better treatment by bosses. There was a large national railroad strike in 1877 with many violent incidents. Thousands of Chicago workers joined the strike in July. By the time it was over, 30 were dead and 200 were hurt. George Pullman became worried that he would have the same problem with his workers, and decided to find a solution.

If he took his workers out of the city, away from the other angry workers, and put them in better homes and safer working areas, Pullman thought, his workers would be thankful, work harder, and never turn against him. Pullman bought 4,000 acres of land south of Chicago on the Illinois Central Railroad and planned a town for his workers. With Pullman running his town like a king, he thought he could uplift the workers and make them better citizens.

[3] A strike is when workers refuse to work until a better or new agreement is reached with the bosses.

The town of Pullman, Illinois, had its first resident on January 1, 1881. By April the factory shops were building and assembling the train cars. The town of Pullman grew from 57 residents in March of 1881 to 11,702 residents in 1892. The homes were made of brick, had plenty of light and fresh air, were provided with gas, and included something that the typical Chicago worker never had—indoor toilets and running water! There were parks and a shimmering lake. Homes had both front and back yards. Garbage was picked up daily. Market Hall was built for the people of Pullman to buy fresh meat and vegetables. An arcade held the Pullman Loan and Savings Bank, a post office, a theater, and a library. Pullman had its own school, hospital, horse stables, and church—everything the workers would ever need. The Hotel

The Arcade Building.

Florence, named for George's favorite daughter, had the only tavern in Pullman. Workers were not allowed in the tavern because Pullman felt that drinking alcohol was bad for them.

Even the factory in Pullman was built to be beautiful, with a landscaped park and a manufactured lake, Lake Vista, in front. Inside, the walls were painted light colors to make it cheerful for the workers. Many windows and skylights made the factory bright with good air flow, unlike the dark, dirty shops where other immigrants and poor people worked at the time.

Do you think Pullman workers were happy or angry? Did living in the town of Pullman stop workers from

An early Pullman erecting shop (in the Detroit shops) shows the airy and bright work space. A young George Pullman is standing in the background.

going on strike? Did the town solve any problems for Pullman?

Nope. The residents became angry that Pullman made all the decisions. The books in the library and the performances at the theater were chosen by Pullman. Inspectors went into homes to make sure they were clean, and company *spotters* spied on residents to make sure they were behaving the way Pullman wanted. Newspapers, public speeches, and town meetings were not allowed. Residents had to rent their homes and were not allowed to own them. The rent was taken right from workers' paychecks, something that is now illegal.

Worst of all, the United States fell into hard times during 1893 and 1894. Many businesses closed, and many people lost their jobs and their money. Pullman didn't want his business to fail, and he didn't want to lose money. To save his company, Pullman paid his workers less. But Pullman didn't charge less rent or lower any prices in the town shops. When workers received their paychecks at the Pullman Loan and Savings Bank, they had little or no pay to show for their work. Workers tried to discuss their problems with Pullman, but he refused to talk to them. On May 11, 1894, 90 percent of Pullman workers went on strike. Federal troops came to Pullman on July 4 to protect the Pullman factory.

Violence occurred between July 5 and 7, ending with injuries, burned railroad cars (but not Pullman cars), and six dead. The strike ended on July 12, 1894, and workers were forced to go back to work.

A hated man, George Pullman died of a heart attack on October 19, 1897, at age 66. He was worth 7.6 million dollars. To prevent angry workers from destroying his body, Pullman was buried in a lead-lined casket beneath concrete and steel rails in Graceland Cemetery in Chicago. At the time of Pullman's death, his company was the largest railroad car maker in the world and 90 percent of all the sleeper cars in North America were rented from Pullman.

The city of Chicago took over the town of Pullman in 1898 when the State of Illinois declared it was *un-American*. Robert Todd Lincoln, son of President

Federal troops protecting the Pullman Factory during the 1894 strike.

Lincoln, took over as president of the Pullman Palace Car Company until 1911. Eventually airlines replaced trains as a faster way to transport people, and the Chicago Pullman plant closed in 1982. Trains are still an important means of travel and shipping in Chicago, but for longer distances, most passengers choose to travel by air. In 2005, Chicago's O'Hare Airport transported more than 76.5 million passengers through its 178 gates.

How was this town supposed to solve immigrant and labor problems?

Did you figure it out?

Collect a star if you figured out that the town of Pullman was a factory town built for employees of the Pullman Palace Car Company. George Pullman hoped that providing a clean, controlled, healthy environment would keep his immigrant workers from striking and make them more respectable citizens.

[STEP BACK TO AN **1880s** COMPANY TOWN.]

The State of Illinois owns and maintains Pullman's Hotel Florence and its factory buildings.

Pullman State Historic Site
11111 S. Forrestville Avenue
Chicago, IL 60628
(773) 660-2341
www.pullman-museum.org

Pullman's Hotel Florence.

[LEARN MORE ABOUT PULLMAN'S UNIQUE HISTORY.]

The Historic Pullman Foundation offers walking tours of the neighborhood and operates a visitors center.

Historic Pullman Visitor Center
11141 S. Cottage Grove Avenue
Chicago, IL 60628
(773) 785-8901
www.pullmanil.org

Typical Pullman row houses.

Investigation 12:

What event did Chicago celebrate?

Find clues on the front and back of this coin to answer the questions:

- Who is on the front of this coin? Can you find any clues to tell you who he is?

- From what country is this coin?
- Why is this man important?
- Which two years can you find on the back of this coin? How are these years related?
- What are the images on the back of the coin?
- Think about all of the words, dates, and images on the coin.
- What important event is this coin honoring?

8244. The G

Now find clues in the picture above:

- What attractions do you see in this picture?
- Where might you see similar attractions today?
- Do the buildings look American or foreign?
- Does the photo look recent or from long ago? How can you tell?
- What type of event might be taking place in this photograph?

Read on to check your guesses.

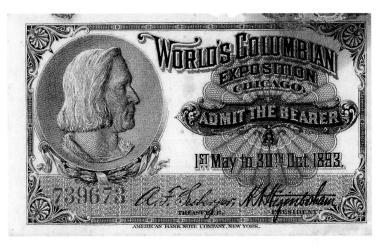

From May 1 to October 30, 1893, the World's Fair, named the Columbian Exposition, was held in Jackson Park in Chicago. A fair this large and well known would bring lots of money and people to the city where it would be held. Chicago's leaders really wanted to show off all of the progress that the city had made after it had burned to the ground only 22 years earlier. In fact, the basic idea behind the exposition was to show off or *expose* new inventions, products, and services. Chicago competed with other big cities like St. Louis and New York City to hold this World's Fair by sending wealthy Chicagoans to argue that Chicago would be the best place for the fair. Charles Dana, an editor for the *New York Sun*, called these Chicagoans "windy politicians," meaning they were full of **bluster**[1] and that they never

---

[1] bluster = roaring or being noisy like the wind, puffed-up talk

stopped bragging. But Chicago wasn't insulted! It took on *The Windy City* as its nickname and won the honor of holding the fair.

A large, vacant, swampy site was chosen on the South Side of the city. A landscaping architect named Fredrick Law Olmstead turned the site into a huge, beautiful park with lagoons and islands. The new park was named Jackson Park, in honor of Andrew Jackson, our country's seventh president from 1829 to 1837.

Daniel Burnham.

Next, Daniel H. Burnham was chosen as the lead architect of the fair. He hired and managed all of the other architects who would design the temporary buildings for the fair. The buildings were made of *staff*, which was a material similar to plaster, containing horse hair. Together, these architects designed and built a Roman and Greek style city, all in white, lit by a new invention—electric lightbulbs! Nicknamed *The White City*, the fair showed visitors how a well-planned city could work with

The Grand Court and Basin of the White City.

electricity, transportation, and an underground sewage system. Everyone hoped that people would be inspired to improve their own neighborhoods after visiting the beautiful and clean White City.

Planners of the fair decided to name it the Columbian Exposition to celebrate the 400th anniversary of Columbus's arrival in the New World and highlight the progress made by America since 1492. The planners were hoping to open the fair in 1892, exactly 400 years after Columbus landed in America, but there was some trouble with the buildings that delayed the opening for another year.

When it opened on May 1, 1893, the fair covered 633 acres and included 65,000 exhibits. Fairgoers were greeted in the Grand Basin by a 65-foot tall golden

Palace of Fine Arts, World's Fair, 1893.

Statue of the Republic, nicknamed *Big Mary* by visitors, sculpted by Daniel Chester French. French was inspired by the Statue of Liberty in New York. More than 200 temporary buildings stood throughout the fair, including 14 great buildings, 45 state buildings, and 46 foreign countries' exhibits.

Great buildings featured exhibits of a similar type, like Machinery Hall, the Transportation Building, and the Palace of Fine Arts. The Women's Pavilion was designed by a 22-year-old architect from Boston, Sophia Hayden. Its exhibits showed all types of women's work, including art, inventions, and discoveries by women. The Women's Pavilion also featured a rooftop garden where the first chocolate brownie was created and served by Bertha Honore Palmer's chef.

Bertha Honore Palmer was president of the Board of Lady Managers for the fair.

States had their own buildings. In the State of Illinois building, visitors discovered an enormous fossil collection, mosaics made of grains and grasses, and a cooking show featuring 100 ways to prepare corn. Only one state building still exists today, the Maine State Building, in Poland Spring, Maine. The building had been constructed in Chicago with granite, slate, and wood sent from Maine. After the fair ended, a family from Maine purchased the Maine Building for $30,000 and had it shipped back to Maine in 16 freight cars!

A foreign exhibit, the Japanese Pavilion, was on a wooded island where guests could buy a cup of tea at the Tea House and sip it in the Japanese gardens and *Ho-o-den*, three buildings designed in the twelfth-, sixteenth-, and eighteenth-century Japanese style (the *Ho-o* is a mythical Japanese bird that can't be destroyed by fire).

To get around the 633-acre fair, people could rent a wheelchair, ride the elevated train, take a Venetian gondola through the lagoons, and even use a steam-powered *Moving Sidewalk*. New products were introduced. Some are still around today, like Cream of Wheat cereal, Juicy Fruit gum, and Cracker Jack caramel popcorn.

The Midway Plaisance, which was not allowed to be officially part of the fair,[2] was like an amusement park with rides, food, dancing girls, and Buffalo Bill's Wild West Show. Similar to Epcot Center at Walt Disney World,[3] on the one-mile Midway Plaisance one could visit foreign villages, sample their cuisine, experience the country's entertainment, and buy products for which the country was famous.

The Ferris wheel was invented for the Columbian Exposition by George Ferris, a bridge builder from Pittsburgh. The previous World's Fair in Paris had the Eiffel Tower, and Chicago's planners really wanted to outdo Paris. This first Ferris wheel reached 264 feet high (compare that to the Ferris wheel now on Navy Pier, which is 150 feet tall), and each of the 36 *gondolas*,

---

[2] Mrs. Bertha Palmer and her Ladies Board of Managers insisted that the Midway was not respectable enough to be part of the official fair.

[3] Walt Disney's grandfather worked at the Columbian Exposition.

or cars, held 60 people. The charge to ride the wheel was 50 cents. That was expensive considering that 50 cents was also the cost to get into the entire fair!

Another very popular attraction on the Midway was a dancer called Little Egypt, who did a dance with veils. Visitors could also see Eskimos, observe native tribes from Africa, and ride a camel, among many other attractions.

Fire destroyed four of the attractions in January 1894, and a few months later more buildings burned to the ground, ruining any chances of reopening the fair for a second year. Any buildings left standing were either torn down or sold. Still, the fair was successful in many ways. Lots of people came to Chicago and spent money for hotels, transportation, food, and shopping. The fair also created many jobs for people. Electricity was shown to be safe, and people began to use it. Neighborhoods were improved and beautified. Some new buildings

were designed in the classical white style that impressed visitors to the fair.

What event did Chicago celebrate?

Did you figure it out?

Collect a star if you thought that Chicago was honoring both the 400th anniversary of Columbus's arrival and Chicago's own progress. The third red star on the city flag represents the Columbian Exposition of 1893.

[**VISIT THE PALACE OF FINE ARTS.**]

The Palace of Fine Arts from the 1893 Columbian Exposition is now the home of the Museum of Science and Industry.

The Museum of Science and Industry
5700 S. Lake Shore Drive
Chicago, IL 60637
(773) 684-1414
www.msichicago.org

The Museum of Science and Industry was built as the Palace of Fine Arts for the 1893 Columbian Exposition.

[**BE A TIME AND SPACE TRAVELER!**]

Explore the Wooded Island behind the Museum of Science and Industry. It was built to be the site of the Japanese Pavilion for the 1893 World's Fair.

Osaka Japanese Garden and Wooded Island
Jackson Park
Behind the Museum of Science and Industry
Between the East and West Lagoons

Museum of Science and Industry from the Japanese gardens on the Wooded Island.

[GAZE UP AT THE *STATUE OF THE REPUBLIC*.]

A 24-foot high copy of the *Statue of the Republic* stands in the Hayes-Richards Circle (6300 South) in Jackson Park. The replica, about one-third the original size, was created by the original sculptor, Daniel Chester French, and was dedicated in 1918 for the twenty-fifth anniversary of the Columbian Exposition.

Investigation 13:

How did Chicago's government finally stop the city's tiniest but deadliest killers?

Find clues in the tables to help you answer the questions:

Cholera Deaths in Nineteenth-Century Chicago	
Year	Cholera Deaths
1849	678
1850	420
1851	216
1852	630
1853	1
1854	1,424
1855	147
1856 - 1865	5
1866	1561
1867	10
1868	0
1869	0
total for 20 years	5092

Typhoid Deaths in Nineteenth-Century Chicago	
Year	Typhoid Deaths
1871	204
1872	524
1873	272
1881	568
1882	462
1890	1,008
1891	1,997
1892	1,489
1893	670
1894	491
1895	518
total for 11 years	8203

- In which years were the most people killed from each disease?
- In which years do deaths increase?
- In which years do deaths decrease?
- What prior knowledge do you have about events occurring in any of these years?
- What types of events might cause an increase or decrease in deaths?

Keep reading and make your inference.

Cholera and typhoid are types of diseases that are caused by drinking **contaminated**[1] water. People in the early 1800s didn't know that germs caused diseases; instead, they thought that bad smells caused diseases. In 1854, Dr. John Snow proved that contaminated drinking water was causing cholera in London, England. Nobody paid attention to Dr. Filippo Pacini in Florence, Italy, when he identified a cholera bacteria the same year. In fact, the world didn't learn that cholera was caused by a germ until Dr. Robert Koch of Germany "discovered" it again in 1884.

---

[1] contaminate = to make something unclean by adding dirt, filth, or bacteria. In Chicago the water was contaminated by dead animals, spoiled food, straw, wood shavings, animal dung, and more. A $3 fine was charged to anyone caught dumping these things into the sewer drains.

If you had been a victim of one of these diseases, you would have felt sudden, painful cramps followed by vomiting and diarrhea. Death by dehydration (the body not containing enough water to function) was common. During 1873, the Board of Health found out that people on average died only 11 hours after first getting sick!

Why did people in Chicago drink unclean water? Before Chicago first became a city in 1834, the residents had no choice but to bring water by bucket from the polluted Chicago River to their homes. As the population boomed, it became too difficult to go back and forth to the Chicago River for water. There were just too many people, so the city built a large public well downtown

In what order do you think these events happened? Which were most likely to solve the water-borne disease problem?
Streets and buildings of all sizes were raised four to ten feet from the level of the river.
A public well was constructed at Hubbard Street and Wabash Avenue for residents to use.
Residents got water directly from the Chicago River by bucket.
The natural flow of the Chicago River was reversed, causing the river to flow backwards and away from Lake Michigan.
Water purification plants are built where wastewater is filtered and cleaned.
Heavy storms wash sewage from the area into the water.
Water is pumped from Lake Michigan to peoples' homes.

for residents to use. Some residents got their water at the well to bring back home, and some paid ten cents a barrel to have the well water delivered to their homes by a cart. But as the city continued to grow, so did pollution in the water supply. Cholera and typhoid kept on spreading and killing Chicagoans.

Chicago's leaders knew they had to find a way to keep Chicagoans healthy. Their first solution was to create a Board of Health in 1835. Health inspectors checked on sick people at home to figure out what made them sick, and then made sick people stay in their homes. Inspectors also made sure market goods were safe to eat and drink, and checked boat crews for disease before they were allowed off their boats.

In 1842, pipes were built 150 feet from Lake Michigan's shore to pump water to the city. This didn't stop people from getting sick. The Chicago River's polluted waters flowed right into Lake Michigan and contaminated the drinking water.

Immigrants were blamed for the diseases. Irish and Norwegian immigrants had arrived to work on the Illinois and Michigan (I&M) Canal between 1836 and 1848. Overcrowded immigrant neighborhoods had the highest number of cholera deaths. Families in these areas lived close together, making it easier to spread disease

George Pullman was hired to raise the city from mud. This illustration shows the Briggs House hotel being lifted.

from one person to the next. When someone was sick, they and their environments were not always cleaned well, and that also helped germs spread to others.

Mud was a big problem. Chicago was built on low land, not much higher than the water level of the river. Squishy, mushy mud kept homes from having basements and the city from having underground sewers or drains. Since there were no sewers, garbage and dirty wastewater was dumped directly into the river, which continued to flow into the city's water supply, Lake Michigan. Yuck!

To solve the water pollution problem, the mud had to be dealt with. Chicago leaders decided to lift the city up from the mud. Streets and sidewalks were raised four to ten feet! Some business and home owners wanted their buildings raised too. A building mover from New York named George Pullman (who later invented the Pullman railroad car) was hired to lift entire blocks of buildings. With the help of about 600 men, even a five-floor, 22,000-ton hotel (filled with guests having lunch!) could be lifted almost five feet, and a new foundation of sand or gravel built underneath it. Once the city was raised from the mud, the first sewers were completed in 1856. Unfortunately, the sewers dumped the dirty water and pollution right into the Chicago River, which still flowed into Lake Michigan. The health problem was not solved, but the sewers did reduce disease a bit—as long as no heavy rains pushed the sewage toward the water pipes in the lake.

In 1865, **slaughterhouses**[2] at the Union Stock Yards began to dump animal waste into the south branch of the Chicago River. Dead, rotting animal parts, blood, grease, and animal manure joined the human waste that was already in the water. Decaying animal parts caused the water of the south branch to bubble with gases, giving this part of the river the name, *Bubbly Creek*. Sewage even formed a thick, greasy crust over the surface of the water that sometimes caught fire. The water in this area of the river was so polluted that even

---

[2] slaughterhouse = a place where animals are killed and cut into pieces to use as meat and other goods

Hog Butcher to the World: Chicago's Stockyards

The Union Stock Yards, built on 320 acres of swampland, opened on December 25, 1865. It was the center of Chicago's meatpacking industry for over 100 years and the most important  meatpacking location in the country for decades.

Miles and miles of railroad tracks delivered live animals to up to 2,300 pens. Thousands of cattle, hogs, and sheep were killed, cleaned, and packaged to sell each day. The property even had a post office, fire station, restaurants, taverns, hotels, and other businesses and services.

The refrigerated train car was invented to send meat from the stockyards to other cities without spoiling. Meatpackers like Philip Armour and Gustavus Swift started companies at the stockyards that are still in business today.

Immigrant men, women, and children worked in the Union Stock Yards. Soon small homes and tenements were built nearby for the workers. In the 1800s, the neighborhood was crowded, poor, and residents suffered from illnesses.

By the time the Union Stock Yards closed in 1971, it had grown to cover 475 acres with 50 miles of road inside and 130 miles of train track surrounding it. The entrance gate designed by Daniel Burnham, at Exchange Avenue and Peoria Street, is all that remains of the stockyards today.

This neighborhood is still called *Back of the Yards*.

today, more than 40 years after the stockyards closed, the water still stinks and bubbles at times.

The city of Chicago decided to build pipes farther out into Lake Michigan to reach cleaner water and pump it back to Chicago. Then an engineer named Ellis Chesbrough had an idea. He thought a tunnel could be dug 60 feet underneath and two miles out into the lake. Cleaner water could be pumped into the city from further out in the lake. It was the area closer to the shore that was very polluted.

The water tunnel was completed in 1867, and a new pumping station brought water to the city. Across the street from the pumping station, a limestone water tower was built which still stands on Chicago and Michigan Avenues today.

The Water Tower was designed by architect W.W. Boyington in 1869. Limestone blocks from Joliet, Illinois, were used to build it.

Four years later, Chicago's leaders had another idea. The Chicago River was contaminating the water supply, so why not force it to flow away from Lake Michigan?

City engineers used the Illinois and Michigan Canal to make the dirty river flow away from Lake Michigan and into the canal. City drinking water was suddenly clean! Towns along the canal, though, did not enjoy having Chicago's stinking sewage and pollution flow through their communities. Would you?

Chicago stayed fairly healthy until 1890, when there was a bad outbreak of typhoid fever. Even though the world now knew that diseases were caused by germs, Chicago's population was still creating more pollution because it was still growing. Soon the I&M Canal could no longer keep the lake clean. Heavy storms continued to wash sewage into the lake. Chicago needed to find a better solution to keep Lake Michigan's waters cleaner.

The Chicago Sanitary District was created in 1889 by the State of Illinois to protect the drinking water.

Today, the Chicago River still flows away from Lake Michigan.

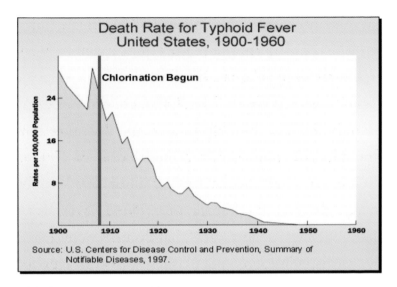

Death Rate for Typhoid Fever
United States, 1900-1960

Chlorination Begun

Rates per 100,000 Population

24

16

8

1900   1910   1920   1930   1940   1950   1960

Source: U.S. Centers for Disease Control and Prevention, Summary of Notifiable Diseases, 1997.

They decided that a larger canal would have to be built to carry Chicago's waste and sewage away from Lake Michigan. Immigrants came from Eastern Europe and African-Americans came from the South to build a canal almost three times as wide and three times as deep as the old I&M Canal. The new canal diggers had an easier time, because steam-powered machines had since been invented for cutting through the earth. In 1900, the 28-mile Sanitary and Ship Canal opened, running alongside the I&M Canal. Seven years later, the Sanitary and Ship Canal was made longer and used for shipping. The flow of the Chicago River was reversed forever, taking Chicago's wastewater and sewage in the opposite direction of Lake Michigan and improving Chicago's drinking water.

Even though wastewater was no longer flowing into

Lake Michigan, the lake waters still contained other types of germs. Even the animals at the Union Stock Yards were thin and unhealthy from drinking the germy water of Bubbly Creek. In 1908, a scientist killed the germs in the water by adding the chemical *chlorine* to it. The stockyard animals became healthier after drinking the cleaner water. In fact, the drinking water at the stockyards was now cleaner than the city's drinking water! Eight years later in 1916, chlorine was added to the city's water supply. Look at the graph on the previous page to see if chlorine helped prevent death by typhoid.

Nearby states became worried that too much water was being lost from Lake Michigan. Compared to other states sharing the lake's water, Chicago had a huge population. The United States government ordered Chicago to start building sewage treatment plants in 1930 to clean the used water and return it to the waterways.

Today, sewage treatment plants clean about 1.5 billion gallons of wastewater (*sewage*) every day and return it to **Chicago area waterways**[3]. The Metropolitan Water Reclamation District of Greater Chicago owns and operates seven sewage treatment plants and 23 pumping stations, and controls about 76 miles of waterways.

---

[3] These waterways are the Chicago River, the Sanitary and Ship Canal, the Cal-Sag Channel, and the North Shore Channel.

The Jardine Purification Plant is the largest water treatment plant in the world.

Unlike sewage treatment plants, water treatment plants are places where water is filtered, cleaned, and sent to people's homes. Lake water for drinking is cleaned in a seven-hour process before it ever reaches Chicago faucets! The James W. Jardine Purification Plant in Chicago is the largest water treatment plant in the world. About one billion gallons of water are cleaned in the plant each day.

As the city grows and changes, so do the methods of keeping its water supply safe. In 1975, the Metropolitan Water Reclamation District began a Deep Tunnel project to help stop stormwater from polluting Chicago's waterways and causing flooding. The Deep Tunnel project consists of 109 miles of tunnels, some as deep as 350 feet down in the limestone. The tunnels direct water to different reservoirs. Later, the reservoir water is cleaned at a plant to make it safe to return to waterways.

How did Chicago's government finally stop its tiniest but deadliest killers?

Did you figure it out?

The killers—cholera and typhoid—were diseases caused by drinking and using contaminated water. To finally stop these diseases from killing Chicago residents, the city reversed the flow of the Chicago River and later began filtering, cleaning, and treating the water with chlorine. Collect your star if you were right!

[**EXPERIENCE NATURE ON THE CANAL.**]

Sewage no longer flows through either the Illinois and Michigan Canal or the Sanitary and Ship Canal. Along the Illinois and Michigan canal today, you can enjoy nature on bike trails, in picnic areas, or even from a canoe. Look for location information on the I&M Canal trail system at the Forest Preserve District of Cook County website: www.fpdcc.com.

[Visit a Chicago River bridgehouse.]

There's a museum devoted to the Chicago River in the southwest bridge tower of one of Chicago's famous movable bridges. Inside? Yes! The museum has five different levels. Start at the base along the river and see the exhibits as you climb to the top.

McCormick Bridgehouse and Chicago River Museum
376 N. Michigan Avenue
Chicago, IL 60601
(312) 977-0227
http://bridgehousemuseum.org

Investigation 14:

How did Daniel Burnham solve overcrowding, business, and transportation problems?

Daniel Burnham had bold plans to solve some of Chicago's big problems. Analyze the clues below, then answer the questions to draw your conclusion:

- What type of work did Burnham do?
- What details can you see in each photo?
- How are the photographs similar?

■ In what way could the photos be related to each other?

■ How could the places in the photographs solve the problems in the city?

Too many people! Chicago's citizens were crowded together, spreading disease and causing crime. These were big problems for the citizens of Chicago in the early 1900s. City leaders needed to find solutions.

Do you remember Daniel Burnham, the famous architect who planned out the White City for the 1893 Columbian Exposition? Well, he had some ideas to solve many of the problems the growing city of Chicago was facing. In 1909, Burnham published his city plan, called the *Plan of Chicago*, and presented it to Chicago on July 4.

Burnham's plan added small neighborhood parks and large public parks like Grant Park to the city of Chicago. Woodlands were saved, or *preserved*, to make *forest preserves* for Chicagoans to enjoy. How

Grant Park.

Chicago, as seen from the Museum Campus.

do you think parks and forest preserves solved the overcrowding, disease, and crime problems?

Here's how:

Having open public spaces like parks meant that homes wouldn't be built in those places. Think about all of the extra people that would be living in the city if every park and forest preserve had homes built on them. Fewer homes mean fewer people. People living crowded together helped spread disease and cause pollution.

Parks and forest preserves would also offer fresh air and free **recreation**[1] for Chicagoans. Chicagoans today still enjoy recreational activities at Chicago's

---

[1] recreation = fun activities during free time

many parks, like tennis, baseball, or basketball. We use their bike paths, or go there just to take a walk. With all of these fun, free, and healthy activities, who has time for crime?

Some of Chicago's favorite parks are built on land that used to be part of Lake Michigan! Grant Park, Northerly Island, and the Museum Campus (where you can visit the Adler Planetarium, the Shedd Aquarium, and the Field Museum of Natural History), Promontory Point in Hyde Park, and Lincoln Park (the site of Lincoln Park Zoo and the Peggy Notebaert Nature Museum) are all built on what used to be part of the lake. Are they floating? Nope. To improve the lakefront for the public, the *Plan of Chicago* dumped *clean* landfill into the lake to create more lakefront land. Clean landfill is made of ash and dirt. Earlier, some of the ash came from the 1871 Great Fire, especially in the area that created Grant Park.

Cha-ching!! That's the sound that business owners in the downtown area wanted to hear—their cash registers busy ringing up sales! The problem was that not enough customers were buying goods and services in the downtown business district, the Loop.

Why not? It wasn't easy to get to the Loop back then. The streets were very narrow and difficult for a new

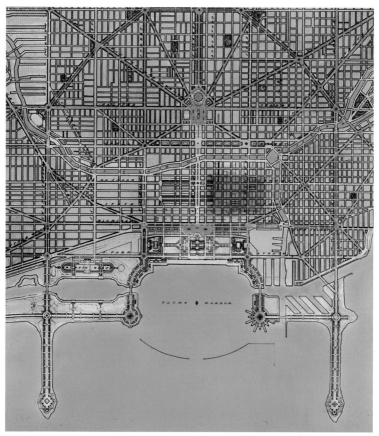

Part of Daniel Burnham's *Plan of Chicago.*

invention—cars—to drive through quickly. Streets in
the city were a confusing maze, sometimes stopping at
a dead end without notice, sometimes changing names.
There were no long streets that went out to the ends
of the city. Cars couldn't pass waterways, and ships
couldn't get to the downtown area to deliver and pick
up goods. Car traffic was slowed or stopped by freight
traffic heading to the docks or rail yards. For the city

to grow and be successful, these problems would have to be solved.

In the plan, streets like Western and Ashland Avenues were widened enough for automobiles, which were larger than horse-drawn buggies. Look at the map of the *Plan of Chicago*. Do you see the long, diagonal streets? Burnham suggested adding even more of these diagonal streets. However, only one diagonal street, Ogden Avenue, was made longer by the plan. These diagonal streets made the drive into the Loop much quicker for people living on the outer edges of the city.

Highways like Lake Shore Drive also made travel by car faster. Small streets were connected and made wider. Some streets were connected by adding bridges over the Chicago River. Two streets, Michigan Avenue and Pine Street, were widened, connected by a bridge, and renamed Michigan Avenue— what is now known as *The Magnificent Mile*. Double-level drives were built along the

Michigan Avenue Bridge.

downtown riverbanks to separate freight traffic from car traffic.

A railway system with tracks and tunnels eventually would be created that would carry both goods (*freight*) and people to and from the business district quickly.

What about travel by water? Chicago was the busiest *port city* in the world, so Burnham included harbors and *piers* to improve business and create jobs. A port city is a city where ships can dock in a harbor to load and unload goods. Piers are platforms that are built from land out into water for ships to use. Burnham planned for piers to be used both for recreation and for shipping by boat. One of Chicago's most famous piers is Navy Pier, now a shopping, dining, and amusement center.

Streets, bridges, railways, and piers helped the city

Recreation Pier postcard, 1921. This is now Navy Pier,
a shopping, dining, and amusement center.

of Chicago make money by making it easy and fast to get people and goods to and from the city.

How did Daniel Burnham solve overcrowding, business, and transportation problems?

Did you figure it out?

The images show that Daniel Burnham's 1909 *Plan of Chicago* gave the city its favorite places to play, work, and shop! Earn a star if you figured out his solutions.

[PAY A VISIT TO THE GRAVE OF **DANIEL BURNHAM** (AND MANY OTHER FAMOUS **CHICAGOANS**).]

Graceland Cemetery
4001 N. Clark Street
Chicago, IL 60613
(773) 525-1105

[CELEBRATE OVER **100** YEARS
OF BURNHAM'S PLAN.]

Daniel Burnham's *Plan of Chicago* turned 100 years old in 2009. Check out the Burnham Plan Centennial website: http://burnhamplan100.lib.uchicago.edu/. Be sure to click on the Kids' Portal in Learning Resources.

The Michigan Avenue Bridge.

Investigation 15:

What is A Century of Progress?

Analyze the artifacts for clues. Then answer the questions:

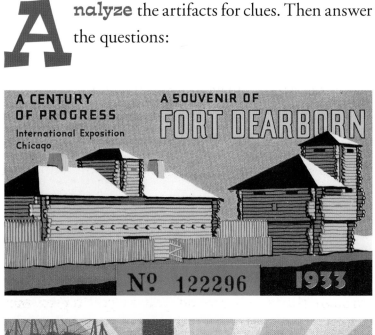

A CENTURY OF PROGRESS
International Exposition
Chicago

A SOUVENIR OF FORT DEARBORN

Nº 122296   1933

1934

1934
A CENTURY OF PROGRESS
CHICAGO

E 377139

GENERAL MANAGER

PRESIDENT

- What years do you see on the artifacts?
- How long is a century?
- What year would have been a century earlier than these dates?
- What does *progress* mean?
- What are the images on the artifacts?
- Why was Fort Dearborn important to Chicago?
- What is the same on all three artifacts?
- From where did these artifacts come?

Brightly colored flags are flapping in the hot Chicago wind above you. The aromas of tasty foods from all over the world tickle your nose. Excited chatter floats through the air all around you as you try to wait patiently to buy your 25-cent children's admission ticket to Chicago's second World's Fair.

In 1933, Chicagoans were thrilled to have their city chosen to host another World's Fair. Times had been hard for all Americans between 1929 and 1939. The entire country was in the Great Depression, a time when many businesses failed and many workers lost their jobs. Without jobs, many people also lost

The Avenue of Flags.

their homes to the banks because they no longer had money to pay back the bank loans on their homes. Farmers lost their farms because they couldn't pay the banks either. Older children had to find jobs to help their families. Lots of people, including kids, became homeless and lived in shacks made of cardboard, pieces of wood, or any other material they could find. These places were known as **Hoovervilles.**[1] But another fair would create jobs for Chicago during these hard times. People who still had jobs could afford to spend money at Chicago businesses. The fair would make life a little more comfortable and enjoyable for Chicagoans during the Great Depression. Chicagoans could forget

[1] Many Americans blamed the country's money problems on their president, President Herbert Hoover, so they named these shack towns "Hoovervilles."

their problems for a little while and have some fun.

The group of city leaders[2] in charge of planning the fair named it *A Century of Progress.* From May 27, 1933, until November 1, 1933, the fair would celebrate 100 years since Chicago had been made a town. The group wanted to show the world all of the progress that had been made in 100 years.

They wanted Americans to see that there was a happy future for them beyond the Great Depression.

Because people were having a hard time with money, only private money was used to pay for the fair, not tax money. Admission tickets stayed the same price as in 1893—40 years before!—50 cents for adults and 25 cents for children. The group wanted the fair to be successful and have many visitors.

424 acres of fairgrounds stretched along the lakefront from 12th Street (now Roosevelt Road) to 39th Street

---

[2] Remember Daniel Burnham and the Columbian Exposition? Both of his sons, Daniel H. Burnham, Jr. and Herbert Burnham, played important roles in A Century of Progress.

This fair was nicknamed *Rainbow City.*

and across the lagoon. Today, as in 1933, the former fairgrounds are the home of Burnham Park, Soldier Field, the Shedd Aquarium, the Adler Planetarium, and the Field Museum. Instead of all-white buildings like the Columbian Exhibition had, the buildings of A Century of Progress were modern and brightly colored to cheer the fairgoers. Glass tubes filled with gas, a new kind of light bulb, glowed along the buildings in greens, yellows, reds, and blues. Neon! This fair was nicknamed *Rainbow City.*

The theme of the fair was science. The main building of the fair was the Hall of Science where visitors could see exhibits and experiments showing new discoveries in medicine, math, physics, and biology. A six-foot-tall

Transparent Man was made in Germany and brought to the Hall of Science to show people how the human body worked. A local hospital charged an extra 25 cents to see living, **premature**[3] babies in incubators. Visitors were fascinated by the tiny babies, who would not have survived without the invention of the incubator.

Other exhibits showed how science could be used to

Looking toward the Shedd Aquarium from Northerly Island.

make useful products like dyes, perfumes, and rubber. Chicago's three museums at the time—the Adler Planetarium, the Field Museum, and the John G. Shedd Aquarium—were also part of the fair. The Shedd Aquarium brought in Australian lungfish for display. Nicknamed *Granddad*, one of these lungfish has lived

---

[3] premature = born too early

to be at least 80 years old and, as of 2012, has survived longer than any fish in all the aquariums of the world.

There was a Travel and Transport Building with a roof that raised and lowered. Surrounding the Travel and Transport Building were new types of trains, tractors, and an 80-foot-tall glass tower of cars. Visitors watched cars being made and tested. There was a fancy Pullman dining car exhibited that was part of the private train of the President of Mexico.

If you were wealthy, you could take a ride in a Goodyear blimp for $3, have a wheelchair pushed by a guide for $1.40 an hour, hire a rickshaw (a cart pulled by a person), or pay $2 to sail on a gondola for an hour. Otherwise you could have traveled the fairgrounds by

The roof of the Travel and Transport Building could be raised and lowered.

foot or in the new 100-person Greyhound bus.[4]

Modern homes were on display like the *House of Tomorrow*, which was a circular glass house with electric doors. People saw new types of building materials, air conditioning, furniture, and appliances like refrigerators, sinks, and cabinets in a rainbow of colors.

Just as in the Columbian Exposition in 1893, each state had its own exhibit. Instead of having separate buildings, this time the states were under one roof in The Parade of States. States demonstrated things for which they were famous. South Dakota, for example, had a model of Mount Rushmore. Because Illinois was hosting the fair, it had its own building. The Illinois Host House featured a three-room exhibit about Abraham Lincoln, including a model of his former living room in Springfield, Illinois.

Foreign countries wanted to show that they were making progress too. They didn't want to be seen as the old-fashioned villages of the 1893 fair. Italy designed a building that looked like an airplane and showed off its progress in science. Nearby stood a 2,000-year-old column shipped from Italy as a gift to Chicago (the column still stands on Northerly Island). It was presented to Chicago by Italian pilot Italo Balbo, who

---

[4] The bus charged ten cents to go from north to south, and 50 cents for a tour of the entire fairgrounds.

flew to Chicago by seaplane and landed on the shores of Lake Michigan.

Because the Midway had made so much money during the Columbian Exposition, the fair organizers made it an official part of A Century of Progress. The Midway included foreign villages as it had for the Columbian Exposition. However, because foreign countries preferred to show modern buildings and exhibits elsewhere in the fair, Chicago built the old-fashioned villages. Americans were hired to dress in the traditional clothes of the foreign countries and work there!

Instead of 1893's Ferris wheel, the *Skyride* was the fair's big, exciting attraction. Visitors paid extra to ride 200 feet over the fair in a rocket-shaped car for a distance of 1,850 feet. Otis elevators brought guests to the top of 628-foot towers—one at each end of the

ride—where they could view the entire fair and see as far away as Indiana, Michigan, and Wisconsin!

The World a Million Years Ago exhibit had visitors carried on a moving platform to the main room where there were giant, moving models of dinosaurs, mammoths, and saber-toothed tigers fighting, eating, or wandering in their natural habitats.

To see how much progress Chicago had made, visitors paid 25 cents extra (ten cents for children) to see a full-sized replica of Old Fort Dearborn complete with fireplaces and two old brass cannons. Models of DuSable's cabin and Father Jacques Marquette's cabin were free to visit inside the fair.

The fair was a success, earning nearly 40 million dollars from admissions and over six million dollars from concessions in its two seasons. A small profit of

$160,000 was shared by the South Park Organization (now part of the Chicago Park District) and organizations that **preserved**[5] fair exhibits like the Museum of Science and Industry, the Art Institute, and the Adler Planetarium.

Lots of money flowed through Chicago during hard times. Thousands of people had work because of the fair, and countless more enjoyed the grand event and forgot about their problems for at least a little while.

It was becoming clear that the city of "I Will" was also a city of "We do" and "We did."

What is A Century of Progress?

Did you figure it out?

A Century of Progress was the World's Fair celebrating Chicago's 100th anniversary and especially highlighting progress made in science and industry in the city, country, and world. The fourth star on the

---

[5] preserve = to save

Chicago flag represents A Century of Progress. Collect a star if you answered the question correctly.

[VISIT THE FAIRGROUNDS TODAY.]

Walk the trails on Northerly Island to find Balbo's Column between Soldier Field and Burnham Harbor. This is the only structure that remains in place today from A Century of Progress.

[VISIT GRANDDAD, THE LUNGFISH.]

John G. Shedd Aquarium
1200 S. Lake Shore Drive
Chicago, IL 60605
(312) 939-2438
http://sheddaquarium.org

[TAKE A FREE TOUR OF THE HOUSE OF TOMORROW AND OTHER WORLD'S FAIR HOMES.]

The House of Tomorrow and other World's Fair homes were bought and moved to Beverly Shores, Indiana. Take a free tour (during the fall only). Reservations required.

Indiana Dunes National Lakeshore
1100 N. Mineral Springs Road
Porter, IN 46304
(219) 395-1882 (information desk)
http://www.nps.gov/indu/historyculture/centuryofprogress.htm

Conclusion

What did it take to make Chicago?

Important waterways, a location in the middle of the country, rich soil, flat land, and animals were all important to Chicago's growth. But courageous and determined *people* were responsible for building and rebuilding the great city known as Chicago. From the first brave settlers starting a community in the swampy wilderness to later Chicagoans withstanding disappointments, disasters, and destruction, to immigrants starting new lives in a new country, Chicagoans have always lived up to the *I Will* motto of their city.

The original two stars on the city flag as designed by Wallace Rice represented the Great Chicago Fire of 1871 and the Columbian Exposition of 1893. The third star was added in 1933 for A Century of Progress World's Fair. A star for Fort Dearborn was added in 1939. White stripes represent parts of the city where people live—north, west, and south. Important waterways are symbolized by the two blue stripes. Some reports say that the stripes are the two branches of the Chicago River, while others name Lake Michigan and the Illinois and Michigan Canal.

How was Chicago made? Now you know all the ingredients, so just add water!

Are You a Chicago Star?

How many stars did you collect?

13–15 stars = A true Chicagoan and visionary! Like a Potawatomi chief, you recognize the greatness of Chicagou's natural resources, landforms, and waterways.

9–12 stars = You're a Chicago champion like DuSable. *DuSable, De Saible.* However he spelled it, he was the first to bring settlers into the area.

6–8 stars = Like William Wells, you're a Chicago hero. Wells bravely fought off attackers using three guns at once during the Fort Dearborn Massacre (now sometimes called the Battle of Fort Dearborn).

4 –5 stars = What a Chicago helper you are like Jane Addams! She helped new residents adjust to a new life, making Chicago a better place.

2–3 stars = A Louis Jolliet you are. He first saw the importance of the Chicago area but never returned to it.

0–1 stars = *What are ya, a New Yorker?*

Index

Image Credits

For images of places with no city and state listed, the location is Chicago, Illinois.

Introduction

1. Chicago flag waving over the Michigan Avenue Bridge, photo by Renee Kreczmer

Investigation 1

1. Log cabin at Goose Lake Prairie State Natural Area, Morris, Illinois, photo by Renee Kreczmer
2. Rivers and Lakes of USA, adapted by Renee Kreczmer from *The National Atlas of the United States of America*
3. Prairie grasses at Goose Lake Prairie, Morris, Illinois, photo by Renee Kreczmer
4. Map of Portage Creek/Mud Lake connection, adapted by Renee Kreczmer from *Chicago and the Continental Divide in 1847* by William Kramer, 1910
5. The Chicago River and Michigan Avenue Bridge today, photo by and courtesy of Charles Osgood, from *Fort Dearborn*, by Jerry Crimmins
6. Goose Lake Prairie, Morris, Illinois, photo by Renee Kreczmer

Investigation 2

1. Portage Creek, Lyons, Illinois, photo by Renee Kreczmer
2. Beaver on display, Isle a la Cache Museum, Romeoville, Illinois, photo by Renee Kreczmer
3. Felted beaver fur top hats on display, Isle a la Cache Museum, Romeoville, Illinois, photo by Renee Kreczmer
4. Map of Portage Creek/Mud Lake connection, adapted by Renee Kreczmer from *Chicago and the Continental Divide in 1847* by William Kramer, 1910
5. Animal pelts displayed at the River Through History festival, Willow Springs, Illinois, photo by Renee Kreczmer
6. Deerskin dresses displayed at the River Through History festival, Willow Springs, Illinois, photo by Renee Kreczmer
7. Isle a la Cache Museum, Romeoville, Illinois, photo by Glen Knoblock, FPDWC staff
8. Wigwams at the River Through History festival, Willow Springs, Illinois, photo by Renee Kreczmer

9. Sculpture of Marquette and Jolliet, Portage Woods, Lyons, Illinois, photo by Renee Kreczmer

Investigation 3
1. De Saible Cabin souvenir booklet, courtesy of the Cheryl R Ganz collection
2. Bronze DuSable bust on Michigan Avenue, photo by Renee Kreczmer
3. South Water Street marker, photo by Renee Kreczmer
5. Michigan Avenue Bridge area, photo by Renee Kreczmer
6. Bronze DuSable bust on Michigan Avenue, photo by Renee Kreczmer
7. Stones from notable world buildings embedded in Tribune Tower, photos by Renee Kreczmer

Investigation 4
1. Drawing of Fort Dearborn, adapted by Renee Kreczmer from *The Story of Old Fort Dearborn*, by J. Currey, 1912
2. Old Fort Wayne, Fort Wayne, Indiana, photo by Renee Kreczmer
3. Inside Old Fort Wayne, Fort Wayne, Indiana, photo by Renee Kreczmer
4. Site of Fort Dearborn, Chicago in 1812 map, adapted by Renee Kreczmer from *The Chicago Massacre of 1812*, by Joseph Kirkland, 1893
5. Rebekah Wells Heald, sketch by Renee Kreczmer
6. Site of Fort Dearborn markers, Michigan Avenue and Wacker Drive, photo by Renee Kreczmer
7. Chicago Landmark plaque, photo by Renee Kreczmer

Investigation 5
1. *Defense* sculpture at Michigan Avenue Bridge, photo by Renee Kreczmer
2. same
3. same
4. same
5. Rebekah Wells Heald & William Wells, sketch by Renee Kreczmer
6. Chicago in 1812 map, adapted by Renee Kreczmer from *The Chicago Massacre of 1812*, by Joseph Kirkland, 1893
7. Who survived and who died?, chart by Renee Kreczmer
8. Old Fort Wayne, Fort Wayne, Indiana, photo by Renee Kreczmer
9. Battle of Fort Dearborn Park, site of massacre on Prairie Avenue, photo by Renee Kreczmer

Investigation 6
1. Population of Chicago by Decades, chart by Renee Kreczmer.

2. Lock 6, Channahon, Illinois, photo by Renee Kreczmer
3. Pickaxe, Gaylord Museum, Lockport, Illinois, photo by Renee Kreczmer
4. Canal scrip, courtesy of the Illinois State Archives
5. Hogan Grain Elevator, Seneca, Illinois, photo by Renee Kreczmer
6. Board of Trade, photo by Renee Kreczmer
7. Packet boat model, Gaylord Building, Lockport, Illinois, photo by Renee Kreczmer
8. Gates, Lock 8, Aux Sable, Illinois, photo by Renee Kreczmer
9. Locktender's house on the I & M Canal, Channahon, Illinois, photo by Renee Kreczmer
10. Gaylord Building, Lockport, Illinois, photo by Renee Kreczmer
11. A packet-boat mule, La Salle, Illinois, photo by Renee Kreczmer
12. Hogan Grain Elevator, Seneca, Illinois, photo by Renee Kreczmer
13. Clarke House, photo by Michael Beasley, courtesy of the Chicago Department of Cultural Affairs

Investigation 7
1. City Charter, Chicago History Museum collection, DN-0058282, photo by the *Chicago Daily News*
2. Corporate seal of Chicago, photo by Renee Kreczmer
3. Council chambers entrance, photo by Renee Kreczmer
4. City Hall interior, photo by Renee Kreczmer
5. City Hall exterior, photo by Renee Kreczmer
6. Journey World, photo by Renee Kreczmer

Investigation 8
1. Melted glass marbles, Chicago History Museum collection, ICHi-61633
2. Wooden balloon frame, photo from Clarke House collection
3. Fire call box on Michigan Avenue, photo by Renee Kreczmer
4. 1853 courthouse plaque, photo by Renee Kreczmer
5. Flammable items, chart by Renee Kreczmer
6. O'Leary cottage, Chicago History Museum collection, DN-0077820, photo by the *Chicago Daily New*s
7. Steamer horse-pulled fire engine on display, Quinn Fire Academy, photo by Renee Kreczmer
8. Firefighter-pulled fire engine on display, Quinn Fire Academy, photo by Renee Kreczmer
9. Stereoview of St. James Hotel ruins, collection of Renee Kreczmer
10. *Pillar of Fire*, Quinn Fire Academy, photo by Renee Kreczmer
11. Water Tower, photo by Renee Kreczmer

12. Pumping Station, photo by Renee Kreczmer

Investigation 9
1. *Regeneration* sculpture, Michigan Avenue Bridge, photo by Renee Kreczmer
2. same
3. Back room [library] in the Old Water Tank, ca. 1873, Chicago Public Library, Special Collections and Preservation Division, CPL Archives
4. Auditorium Building, photo by Renee Kreczmer
5. City skyline from Soldier Field, photo by Renee Kreczmer
6. Auditorium Building, photo by Renee Kreczmer
7. Santa Fe Building, photo by Renee Kreczmer

Investigation 10
1. "The Stranger at our Gate" political cartoon from *The Ram's Horn* magazine, by Frank Beard, 1896, Billy Ireland Cartoon Library & Museum, The Ohio State University
2. Immigration chart, adapted by Renee Kreczmer from data adapted from *Ethnic Chicago: A Multicultural Portrait*, 4th Edition, edited by Melvin G Holli and Peter d'A. Jones.
3. Ethnic neighborhood, photo by Renee Kreczmer
4. Ethnic neighborhood, photo by Renee Kreczmer
5. Children playing in alley behind tenement housing: photographer unknown, ca. 1900, JAMC_0000_0193_0296, Jane Addams Hull-House Photograph Collection, University of Illinois at Chicago Library
6. View of Hull-House with Butler Art Gallery to the left and the Smith building to the right: photographer unknown, ca. 1898, JAMC_0000_0132_0150, Jane Addams Hull-House Photograph Collection, University of Illinois at Chicago Library
7. Hull-House Museum, photo by Renee Kreczmer

Investigation 11
1. Map of Pullman, 1885, Bertha Ludlam Research and Archive Collection, Pullman State Historic Site
2. The Pioneer, Pullman's first sleeping car, Bertha Ludlam Research and Archive Collection, Pullman State Historic Site
3. Inside a Palace Car, Bertha Ludlam Research and Archive Collection, Pullman State Historic Site
4. A Pullman porter, Bertha Ludlam Research and Archive Collection, Pullman State Historic Site
5. The Arcade Building, Bertha Ludlam Research and Archive Collection, Pullman State Historic Site

6. An early Pullman erecting shop, Bertha Ludlam Research and Archive Collection, Pullman State Historic Site
7. Federal troops protecting the Pullman Factory during the 1894 strike, Bertha Ludlam Research and Archive Collection, Pullman State Historic Site
8. Hotel Florence, photo by Renee Kreczmer
9. Pullman row houses, photo by Renee Kreczmer

Investigation 12
1. Columbian half-dollar (front), collection of Renee Kreczmer
2. Columbian half-dollar (back), collection of Renee Kreczmer
3. Ferris Wheel stereoview, collection of Renee Kreczmer
4. Columbian Expo ticket, collection of Renee Kreczmer 5. Daniel Burnham portrait, September 1893. C.D. Morse (Chicago) [photographer]. Daniel Burnham collection, Ryerson and Burnham Archives, The Art Institute of Chicago. Digital File #194301.090619-01 © The Art Institute of Chicago.
7. Fine Arts Palace stereoview, collection of Renee Kreczmer
8. Bertha Honore Palmer, collection of Renee Kreczmer
9. Ferris wheel at Columbian Exposition, collection of Renee Kreczmer
10. Museum of Science and Industry, photo by Renee Kreczmer
11. Museum of Science and Industry from Japanese gardens, photo by Renee Kreczmer
12. Replica of *The Statue of the Republic*, photo by Renee Kreczmer

Investigation 13
1. Cholera Deaths in Nineteenth-Century Chicago, chart compiled by Renee Kreczmer
2. Typhoid Deaths in Nineteenth-Century Chicago, chart compiled by Renee Kreczmer
3. Chart of steps taken in order to solve problems of water-borne diseases in Chicago, chart by Renee Kreczmer
4. Raising of Briggs House, photo from the collection of the Pullman State Historic Site
5. Union Stock Yards gate, photo by Renee Kreczmer
6. Water Tower, photo by Renee Kreczmer
7. Chicago River flowing under the Michigan Avenue Bridge, photo by Renee Kreczmer
8. Death Rate for Typhoid Fever, United States, 1900–1960, chart from the Washington State Department of Health-Division of Environmental Health-Office of Drinking Water-Constituent Services Section and U.S. Center for Disease Control

9. Entrance to the Jardine Water Purification Plant, photo by Renee Kreczmer
10. Bridgehouse Museum, courtesy of Ozana Balan-King, Friends of the Chicago River

Investigation 14
1. Daniel Burnham portrait, September 1893. C.D. Morse (Chicago) [photographer]. Daniel Burnham collection, Ryerson and Burnham Archives, The Art Institute of Chicago. Digital File #194301.090619-01 © The Art Institute of Chicago.
2. Clockwise: Forest Glen Woods, Grant Park, Pullman cash register, Chicago River, Northerly Island, photos by Renee Kreczmer
3. Grant Park, photo by Renee Kreczmer
4. Chicago, as seen from the Museum Campus, photo by Renee Kreczmer
5. "Plan of Chicago," Pl. 110, Chicago, Illinois, c. 1908. Daniel H. Burnham and Edward H. Bennett [architects]. A.G. McGregor (Chicago) [photographer], Rose Kingwill (Chicago) [colorer]. Ryerson and Burnham Archives, The Art Institute of Chicago. Digital File #15102 © The Art Institute of Chicago.
6. Michigan Avenue Bridge, photo by Renee Kreczmer
7. Navy Pier/Recreation Pier [postcard], 1921, Chicago Public Library, Special Collections and Preservation Division, CCW 6.47
8. Graceland Cemetery sign, photo by Renee Kreczmer
9. Michigan Avenue Bridge, photo by Renee Kreczmer

Investigation 15
1. Fort Dearborn exhibit ticket stub, collection of Renee Kreczmer
2. Century of Progress ticket stub, collection of Renee Kreczmer
3. Century of Progress souvenir ashtray, collection of Renee Kreczmer
4. Avenue of Flags, *Official Pictures in Color*
5. "I Will" poster: creator unknown, ca. 1933–1934, COP_17_0023_00000_049, Century of Progress Records, 1927–1952, University of Illinois at Chicago Library
6. Night Panorama, *Official Pictures in Color*
7. Looking toward the Shedd Aquarium from Northerly Island, photo by Renee Kreczmer
8. Travel & Transport Building, *Official Pictures in Color*
9. Italian Pavilion, *Official Pictures in Color*
10. Foreign Villages, *Official Pictures in Color*

Conclusion
1. Chicago flag over Michigan Avenue Bridge, photo by Renee Kreczmer

Bibliography

Addams, Jane, and Residents of Hull-House. *Hull-House Maps and Papers: A Presentation of Nationalities and Wages in a Congested District of Chicago, Together with Comments and Essays on Problems Growing Out of the Social Conditions.* Champaign, IL: University of Illinois, 2007.

American Chemistry Council. "CDC Calls Drinking Water Chlorination a Significant Public Health Advance." Chlorine Chemistry. Accessed March 25, 2012. http://chlorine.americanchemistry.com/Safer-Water.

Autodesk, Inc. "World's Largest Water Treatment Plant Optimizes Procedures Based on ALGOR Fluid Flow Results." Accessed March 25, 2012. http://www.algor.com/news_pub/cust_app/jardine/jardine.asp.

Avalon Project—Documents in Law, History and Diplomacy. "The Treaty of Greenville 1795." Accessed December 26, 2009. http://avalon.law.yale.edu/18th_century/greenvil.asp.

Bolotin, Norman, and Christine Laing. *The World's Columbian Exposition.* Champaign, IL: University of Illinois, 1992.

Calloway, Colin G. *New Worlds for All: Indians, Europeans, and the Remaking of Early America.* Baltimore, MD: Johns Hopkins University Press, 1997.

Canal Corridor Association. *I&M Canal Passage Driving Tour.* Chicago: Canal Corridor Association, 2002.

Chicago Architecture Info. "The Home Insurance Building." Accessed December 26, 2009. http://www.chicagoarchitecture.info/Building.php?ID=3168.

Chicago Department of Aviation. "Chicago Department of

Aviation - History." Accessed March 25, 2012. http://www.
flychicago.com/About/History/Default.aspx.

Chicago Department of Health Reports. Publication. Chicago,
1849–1910.

Chicago History Museum. Accessed November 28, 2009. http://
www.chicagohs.org.

Chicago Metropolis 2020. *The Plan of Chicago: A Regional Legacy.*
Chicago: Chicago Metropolis 2020, 2008.

Chicago Public Library. "Chicago Facts." Accessed December 26,
2009. http://www.chipublib.org/cplbooksmovies/cplarchive/
facts/index.php.

Chicago Tribune (ProQuest Historical Newspapers). Indiana
University Libraries. Accessed November 27, 2009. http://www.
libraries.iub.edu/index.php?pageId=400&resourceId=1577184.

City of Chicago. "Chicago Government." Accessed December 26,
2009. http://www.cityofchicago.org/city/en/chicagogovt.html.

Clarke House Museum. Accessed December 29, 2009. http://
www.clarkehousemuseum.org.

College of Micronesia-FSM. "The History of Science Microscopes,
Social Statistics and Cholera." Accessed October 21, 2009.
http://www.comfsm.fm/socscie/histchol.htm.

Conzin, Michael, Douglas Knox, and Dennis Cremin. *1848
Turning Point for Chicago, Turning Point for the Region.* Chicago:
Newberry Library, 1998.

Cook County Illinois Genealogy Trails. "Finding Illinois
Ancestors: Fort Dearborn." Accessed December 26, 2009. http://
genealogytrails.com/ill/cook/ftdearborn.html.

Crimmins, Jerry. *Fort Dearborn.* Evanston, IL: Northwestern
University Press, 2008.

Currey, J. Seymour. *The Story of Old Fort Dearborn.* Chicago: A.C.
McClurg, 1912.

Curtis, Jennie. "The Parable of Pullman." Illinois Labor

History Society. Accessed March 25, 2012. http://www.
illinoislaborhistory.org/articles/223-the-parable-of-pullman.
html.

Emporis.com. "Buildings in Chicago." Accessed December 26,
2009. http://www.emporis.com/en/wm/ci/bu/sk/?id=101030.

First People of America and Canada. "Treaty with The
Ottawa, etc.—August 24, 1816." Accessed December
26, 2009. http://www.firstpeople.us/FP-Html-Treaties/
TreatyWithTheOttawaetc1816.html.

Forest County Potawatomi. "Forest County Potawatomi—Treaty
of Chicago." Accessed December 26, 2009. http://www.
fcpotawatomi.com/index.php/Treaties/Treaty-of-Chicago.html.

Galbraith, Michael. E-mail message to author, September 21, 2009.

Ganz, Cheryl R. *The 1933 Chicago World's Fair: A Century of
Progress.* Champaign: University of Illinois, 2008.

Gilman, Carolyn. *Where Two Worlds Meet.* St. Paul, MN:
Minnesota Historical Society, 1982.

Grossman, James R., Ann Durkin Keating, and Janice L. Reiff,
eds. *The Encyclopedia of Chicago.* Chicago: University of
Chicago, 2004.

Heath, William. *Blacksnake's Path: The True Adventures of William
Wells.* Westminster, MD: Heritage Books, 2009.

Hill, Libby. E-mail message to author, December 20, 2010.

Historic Pullman Foundation. Accessed November 28, 2009.
http://www.pullmanil.org/town.htm.

Holli, Melvin G., and Peter D'A. Jones, eds. *Ethnic Chicago: A
Multicultural Portrait.* 4th ed. Grand Rapids, MI: William B.
Eerdmans, 1995.

Hubbard, Gurdon S. *The Autobiography of Gurdon Saltonstall
Hubbard, Pa-pa-ma-ta-be, "The Swift Walker."* Grand Rapids,
MI: Black Letter, 1981.

Illinois Department of Natural Resources. "Of Time And The

River: 12,000 Years of Human Use of the Illinois River."
Accessed October 21, 2009. http://oftimeandtheriver.org.

James, Edmund, Ph.D., ed. *The Charters of the City of Chicago.*
Chicago: University of Chicago, 1808.

Jane Addams Hull-House Museum. "Urban Experience in
Chicago: Hull-House and Its Neighborhoods, 1889–1963."
Accessed November 26, 2009. http://www.uic.edu/jaddams/
hull/urbanexp.

Johnson, Geoffrey. "True Story of the Deadly Encounter at Fort
Dearborn." *Chicago Magazine.* Dec. 2009. Accessed January
21, 2012. http://www.chicagomag.com/Chicago-Magazine/
December-2009/The-True-Story-of-the-Deadly-Encounter-at-
Fort-Dearborn/index.php?cparticle=2.

Kirkland, Joseph. *The Chicago Massacre of 1812.* Chicago: Dibble,
1893.

Lewis, Lloyd. *Chicago: The History of Its Reputation.* New York
City: Blue Ribbon, 1929.

Lienhard, John H. "No. 779: Balloon Frame Houses." University
of Houston. Accessed December 26, 2009. http://www.uh.edu/
engines/epi779.htm.

McHenry County Civil War Roundtable. "Civil War in McHenry
County. Galena and Chicago Union Railroad." Accessed
November 28, 2009. http://www.mchenrycivilwar.com/
Local%20History/Railroad.html.

McLear, Patrick E. "The Galena and Chicago Union Railroad: A
Symbol of Chicago's Economic Maturity." *Journal of the Illinois
State Historical Society* 73.1 (1980): 17–26.

National Atlas. "Printable Maps - Reference." Accessed March 25,
2012. http://www.nationalatlas.gov/printable/reference.html.

National Park Service, U.S. Department of the Interior. *Archeology:
Illinois and Michigan Canal National Heritage Corridor.*

Natta, Larry. *Canal Town.* Ottawa, IL: Heritage Corridor, 2000.

Office of the Secretary of State. "Early Chicago, 1833–1871." Illinois Secretary of State Jesse White. Accessed March 25, 2012. http://www.cyberdriveillinois.com/departments/archives/teaching_packages/early_chicago/home.html.

Ossewaarde, Gary. "'The Republic' in Jackson Park." Hyde Park-Kenwood Community Conference Home. Accessed March 24, 2012. http://www.hydepark.org/parks/jpac/jprepublic.htm#story.

Paral, Rob. *The Metro Chicago Immigration Fact Book*. Chicago: Institute for Metropolitan Affairs, Roosevelt University, 2003.

Pierce, Bessie Louise, and Joe Lester Norris, eds. *As Others See Chicago:Iimpressions of Visitors, 1673-1933*. Chicago, IL: University of Chicago Press, 1933.

Pierce, Bessie Louise. "Pullman's First Car." ADENA. Accessed March 25, 2012. http://www.adena.com/adena/usa/hs/hs13.htm.

Poland Spring Preservation Society. "Maine State Building, Poland Spring, Maine." Accessed March 24, 2012. http://www.polandspringps.org/maine_state_building.html.

Pullman State Historic Site. Accessed November 28, 2009. http://www.pullman-museum.org.

Quaife, Milo Milton. *Chicago and the Old Northwest 1673–1835*. Champaign, IL: University of Illinois, 2001.

Reardon, Patrick T. "Historian: Zell deal 'a great paradox'." Chicago Tribune. Accessed March 25, 2012. http://www.chicagotribune.com/business/chi-070402tribune-history,0,3204572.story.

Shedd [John G.] Aquarium. "Granddad: The Aquarium's Oldest Fish." Accessed March 24, 2012. http://www.sheddaquarium.org/granddad.html.

Sheffield Industrial Museums Trust. "The Bessemer Converter." Accessed March 25, 2012. http://simt.co.uk/kelham-island-museum/bessemer-converter.

Swenson, John F. "Early Chicago—Chicago History." Accessed December 26, 2009. http://www.earlychicago.com.

UCLA School of Public Health, Department of Epidemiology. "Who First Discovered Cholera?" Accessed December 26, 2009. http://www.ph.ucla.edu/EPI/snow/firstdiscoveredcholera.html.

Union Pacific Corporation. "Railroading Turns 160 Years Old in Chicago." Accessed November 28, 2009. http://www.uprr.com/newsinfo/releases/heritage_and_steam/2008/1022_chicago160.shtml.

Wiltz, Teresa. "The Chicago Fire." Chicago Tribune. Accessed March 24, 2012. http://www.chicagotribune.com/news/politics/chi-chicagodays-fire-story,0,2790977.story.

Young, David. "The Galena and Chicago Union." Chicago Tribune. Accessed March 25, 2012. http://www.chicagotribune.com/news/politics/chi-chicagodays-galenaunion-story,0,7617713.story.

Acknowledgments

Writing a Chicago history book for kids was a notion that had never occurred to me, even though there was desperate need of one. Always on the lookout for appropriate Chicago materials, I was thrilled when I heard that Lake Claremont Press was planning a children's history book, then shocked when publisher Sharon Woodhouse asked me to write it! I'd like to thank her for extending the opportunity to me and initiating the idea. Also, I am grateful to the Schulte and Shaw families for, among other things, connecting me with Lake Claremont Press.

To my entire family (aunts, uncles, cousins, in-laws) and close friends who supported and encouraged me through this project, I appreciate you more than I could ever put into words. Thanks especially to Dad and Mom (Larry and Mary), who eagerly accompanied me to the historic sites, calculated math for charts, drove me around, collected information, proofread chapters, and tried to make my life as easy as possible during work on this book; Aunt Sherry who helped me with her expert production knowledge; to my grandparents, Reno Cracco and Sophia Kreczmer, who always have such lively stories of the 1930s; and to my little brother, my comrade, you are the talented writer in the family. I love you all.

Joseph Kallas deserves huge thanks for arranging and attending summer meetings to find buyers for the book, and offering his suggestions, encouragement, and incredible support for this project. Martin Moe and Teresa Garate—thank you for helping to make Chicago history the third grade curriculum for the Chicago Public Schools. For their patience and support, thank you to Chris Munns, Melissa Raich, my students, and my colleagues.

To all the smart, talented people who helped me create this book by sharing their knowledge, work, or collections—I am so grateful for your input. Thank you Ozana Balan-King of Friends of the Chicago River; Debra Shore of the Metropolitan Water Reclamation District; Donna Lynch from the Washington State Department of Health; Cheryl Ganz and the Smithsonian; Shauna Metee, officer for the CDC; all the Fort Wayne Historians of Fort Wayne and Detroit: Ken Song, Jeremy Bevard, Adam Lovell, Michael Galbraith, Randy Elliot, and all the dedicated volunteers of Historic Fort Wayne, Inc.; Friends of the Chicago Portage; Lesley Martin at the Chicago Historical Society Research Center; Jerry Crimmins, author of the excellent *Fort Dearborn* novel; Charles Osgood, the awesome photographer; Mike Wagenbach, Linda Beierle Bullen, and all our friends from Pullman; Laura Kirin of the Forest Preserve District of Will County; the staff at the Hull-House Museum; the volunteers at the Des Plaines Valley Rendezvous; Mark Harmon and the volunteers at the Gaylord Building; Mark MacLean; Peggy Glowacki; Manny Soto and Steve Scott from Quinn Fire Academy; and all the historians I've met at historic sites and events over the years, so eager to share their knowledge. Historians rock! Thank you for your help.

Finding images was more difficult than imagined. Thanks to Leslie and Mick, Val, Bryan, Dave H., David D., Aunt Sherry, and the girl who almost missed her bus to help me take a photo on Belmont.

About the Author

A student and teacher of Chicago's exciting history for 17 years, Renee Kreczmer is a social studies teacher for the Chicago Public Schools. She has attended educational workshops with the Chicago Architecture Foundation and Chicago History Museum; completed coursework in Chicago history at Roosevelt University; and frequented countless museums, historic sites, history tours, and historical reenactments in her 17-year effort to discover the best materials and methods for teaching the mandated Chicago curriculum to her third-grade students. She shares much of that knowledge and experience in this book. Ms. Kreczmer has also assisted in social studies curriculum development for the Chicago Public Schools.

"Learning about Chicago is so cool!"

—Arielle C.

"I feel great learning about Chicago. It's so fascinating!"

—Claire C.

"I'm glad Ms. Kreczmer is teaching us this. Chicago is very interesting."

—Kyle C.

"Investigating Chicago is fun, so you should try it for once...and learn a lot about Chicago history."

—Justin C.

"Truly and honestly I think I am really going to learn a lot. I love, love, love learning about Chicago. I even sometimes educate my parents about Chicago!"

—Nicole H.

"Investigating Chicago is interesting, fun, and you can experience life [as it was] before."

—Aphrodite O.

"I think investigating Chicago is very interesting, fun, and awesome. My favorite part of investigating was learning about the canal."

—Kat P.

"Investigating Chicago is very cool because you get to learn about the native culture, artifacts, and their way of survival."

—Miles S.

"I love Social Studies because Ms. Kreczmer makes it so fun instead of so boring."

—Eliza W.